D0097906

ON TARGET

ON TARGET

HOW TO CONDUCT EFFECTIVE BUSINESS REVIEWS

Michele L. Bechtell

BK Berrett-Koehler Publishers, Inc.
San Francisco

Berrett-Koehler Publishers, Inc.
235 Montgomery Street, Suite 650
San Francisco, CA 94104
Tel: (415) 288-0260 Fax: (415) 362-2512 www.bkconnection.com

ORDERING INFORMATION

Quantity sales. Special discounts are available on quantity purchases by corporations, associations, and others. For details, contact the "Special Sales Department" at the Berrett-Koehler address above.

Individual sales. Berrett-Koehler publications are available through most bookstores. They can also be ordered direct from Berrett-Koehler:
Tel: (800) 929-2929; Fax: (802) 864-7626; www.bkconnection.com

Orders for college textbook/course adoption use. Please contact Berrett-Koehler: Tel: (800) 929-2929; Fax: (802) 864-7626.

Orders by U.S. trade bookstores and wholesalers. Please contact Publishers Group West, 1700 Fourth Street, Berkeley, CA 94710.
Tel: (510) 528-1444; Fax (510) 528-3444.

Production Management: Michael Bass & Associates

Printed in the United States of America

Printed on acid-free and recycled paper that is composed of 85% recovered fiber, including 15% post consumer waste.

Library of Congress Cataloging-in-Publication Data

Bechtell, Michele L., 1956–
On Target: how to conduct effective business reviews / by Michele L. Bechtell.
p. cm.
Includes bibliographical references and index.
ISBN 1-57675-171-6
1. Management by objectives. 2. Organizational effectiveness. 3. Strategic planning. 4. Business planning. I. Title: Effective business reivews. II Title.

HD30.65 .B43 2001
658.4'02–dc21 2001052609

First Edition

06 05 04 03 02 10 9 8 7 6 5 4 3 2 1

With tender love and deep gratitude, I dedicate this book to my wonderful husband, Edward.

CONTENTS

LIST OF ILLUSTRATIONS

ACKNOWLEDGMENTS

Without God's help and inspiration, this book would not be possible. Many thanks go to the numerous, enthusiastic, and talented individuals who influenced this book from contributing practical examples to providing valuable content and editorial suggestions. Specifically, I thank Mark Arnold, Pete Babich, Frank Ferraco, Louise Firth, Edward Fritzi, Don Mattes, Gerard O'Connor, Steven Piersanti, and Rolf Weber for their support and encouragement throughout this project. Finally, I express deep appreciation to the many organizations and students of management throughout the world who have invited me to work with them to develop new management techniques in the spirit of continuous learning.

ON TARGET

INTRODUCTION

DON'T DESPAIR!

YOU CAN DO IT

This book shows how to conduct powerful reviews to reliably achieve ambitious business objectives. It shows how to put any plan into action for rapid intentional results, not once, but repeatedly. It looks beyond incremental improvement to show you how to make quantum leaps in performance for dramatic strategic advantage. It is about predictably achieving what you set out to do.

Many people routinely fail to achieve their stated business objectives. They formulate strategic plans, annual plans, operating plans, and financial plans, and they assign individual goals to support high-level objectives. Yet, their predictions fail to come true with alarming regularity. If they do meet plan, they really don't know how to repeat the success.

What is the evidence? A general lack of success can be diagnosed by a visual inspection of historical performance versus plan. Whether it is growth, net

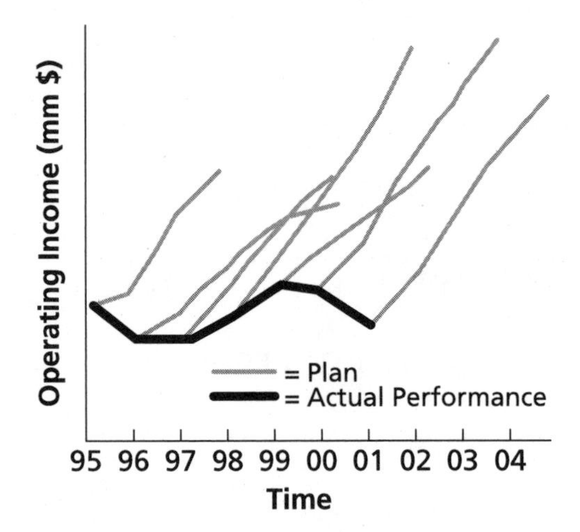

FIGURE I-1 A Typical History of UnMet Expections Looks Like a Feather Chart

operating profits, market share, or customer loyalty, many companies exhibit a history of unmet expectations that reveals a chronic inability to reliably deliver intended outcomes. (Figure I-1 illustrates such a typical performance history.)

If hitting targets is perceived as essential for survival, then why do so many organizations fail to achieve their desired goals and objectives? One answer lies in inadequate review. Many people blame their failed objectives on the quality of their initial strategies or the people on whom they depend. Truth is, most plans fail neither in design nor capability; they fail during implementation.

Frequent effective review is a critical implementation behavior. Yet, in many companies, there is no structure, no discipline, and no systematic follow-up. Objectives are poorly defined, rarely reviewed, and they receive inconsistent leadership attention. There is simply no professional process by which to improve. In short, the leadership lacks a method or system to achieve *any* plan.

Inadequate review contributes to many missed objectives. Early failures go unnoticed and therefore uncorrected. Take a moment to examine the review practices in your own organization:

- What vital *few* gaps, no more than three, must be closely monitored and controlled over the next twelve months to make dramatic progress toward your vision? Does everyone agree on these goals? If not, why not? What are you doing about it?
- Do individual goals *add up* to collectively deliver these high-level objectives? How do you know?
- How *often* do you review factual progress? At the end of the year? Four times a year?
- Precisely how far away from annual commitments are people right now? How do you know? Can you *verify* it?
- Which agreed-on methods are not being implemented? When did you find out? What corrective *actions* did you take? Are the new "improved" methods failing, too?
- Do people report using a *common,* immediately understandable format? Or do reporting styles differ by region, function, and personality?

If you are like many people, you may not know the answers to these questions, feel overwhelmed by the questions, or feel troubled by your answers. Or perchance, by the time you discovered the answers to these questions, it was too late to take appropriate action. Many leaders fail to take the time to clarify the vital few measures of success. They conduct infrequent reviews and therefore fail to detect early warning signs. They remain ignorant about where they stand on critical business parameters and how fast they are changing familiar yet dysfunctional behaviors. And they fail to verify adequate intervention. By receiving too little information, too late, they lose flexibility and power.

FREQUENT REVIEW ACCELERATES DESIRED OUTCOMES

Today, we can ill afford the time to do things twice. Incomplete or inadequate plans, nonadherence to plan, the nonintegration of all business units, insufficient corrective action, and disagreements on direction, always cost time, money, and strategic advantage.

Frequent reviews can eliminate these unnecessary errors and delays. When we continually track progress, we can readily:

- determine precise location,
- detect early deviations from expectation,
- study the root cause of disappointing results,
- install timely, appropriate corrective action, and
- adjust the plan to reflect new developments.

Such routine practices ensure rapid strategy implementation and reliable results.

The key words are *rapid, strategy,* and *implementation.* Frequent review can answer such important questions as: Are we achieving our stated objectives *quickly* enough? Are we focused on the *most important* issues for competitive advantage? Are we *doing* what we said we wanted to do? Prompt, thorough answers to these questions increase our probability of success in implementing any plan.

EFFECTIVE REVIEW IS A CORE LEADERSHIP COMPETENCY

Effective review can accelerate every change process. Unfortunately, many people experience the review as a stressful, unpredictable, irrelevant event often disconnected from high-level strategic priorities. This is understandable. Too often, the business review is confused with a sporadic review of *personnel* that focuses primarily on individual accomplishments. Superiors spend little or no time to factually analyze or modify the false assumptions or inadequate information that led people astray in the first place. And, often the wrong individuals get blamed for disappointing results.

Without intending to, many leaders create an environment of "learned helplessness" in which individuals lack a personal connection to collective outcomes. These leaders primarily monitor financial measures of success and adherence to budget. But traditional financial outcomes are indirectly influenced by many individuals, often overemphasize short-term performance, and communicate the success of numerous choices and strategies after the fact. They fail to communicate the critical leading, often nonfinancial, *causal factors* that individuals can and must monitor and control to deliver desired outcomes.

Leaders such as the ones described earlier often espouse the need for accountability at all levels of the enterprise. Yet, in their behavior they reject the notion that accountability can be learned. They hire intelligent creative people and assign them aggressive annual goals. Then, they provide no explicit guidelines on how to succeed. They create a culture that teaches clever people the only way to succeed is the school of guesswork. We achieve much better results when we define and enforce a reliable professional process in which everyone can track factual performance, test assumptions, and experiment with new methods.

To leverage the power of review for best effect, wise leaders shift from conducting the performance review as a stand-alone event focused on lagging outcomes and personnel to managing the review as a disciplined *process* by which the organization transforms itself to achieve new levels of performance. They look beyond the strategic planning workshop event, the specific measures or paper plan, and the varied skills of personnel, to identify and practice the critical few *behaviors* required to achieve any plan.

CONTROL THE REVIEW PROCESS

Effective review is fundamentally a controlled change process. It is a transforming process, an adapting process, one that increases the likelihood of accomplishing goals and objectives. The input is a set of behaviors producing current levels of performance. The desired output is a new set of behaviors producing new levels of performance consistent with the vision. The steps between map the cause-and-effect relationships between the activities we do and the results that we achieve.

As our environment changes, so do our precise goals and objectives. Thus, a reliable review process is a self-correcting process with no beginning and no end that keeps the plan aligned with changes in the environment and activity aligned with the plan. Managed properly, it creates a systematic governance mechanism to modify routine behaviors continually to achieve new levels of performance.

Despite a stated focus on process control, the review process in many companies resembles a collection of sporadic events, not coordinated steps in a continuous organizational transformation. In many small businesses, the progress review is nonexistent or anecdotal at best. In large organizations, reviews typically devolve into an unmanageable information mess:

- Reporting formats differ by geography, hierarchical level, functional specialty, and/or management style;
- Communications range from oral reports to written memorandums to elaborate audiovisual presentations;
- The frequency of review fluctuates from annual to weekly to none at all.

These and other variations in behavior waste precious time and energy. Best practices become confused with irresponsible ones. And local discoveries fail to inform important decisions elsewhere in the organization.

A controlled process always outperforms an ad hoc process in effectiveness, reliability, and speed. This axiom holds true for the review process. What to report, when to report, and how to best use shared time is critical to rapid strategy deployment.

For this reason, wise leaders design their review process as a *continually improving* process. From month to month and from year to year, they take the time to discover which planning, implementation, and review techniques worked and why. Then they document, standardize, and continually improve the "best agreed-on" practices to minimize unnecessary errors and delays.

Effective review is not difficult. It is just different from the way many leaders have conducted business in the past. It demands honest attention to the contradictions between common sense, what we believe we are doing, and factual behavior. We improve our likelihood of success when we specify and control such things as the number of objectives, the frequency of review, the reporting format, and procedural response to deviations from expectation. Unmanaged, these and other variables erode the organization from within. Controlled, they can become powerful tools to accelerate any change process for dramatic effect. Conducting effective reviews becomes a leadership choice.

YOU CAN DO IT!

The most common causes of failed objectives are internally created and can be internally corrected with disciplined review. That is the simple message of *On Target.* In three parts, it shows how anyone can standardize and control review behavior to accelerate any change process. Specifically, it shows how to:

Choose what to review to focus attention on the critical few success factors (Part I).

Conduct frequent reviews to detect early warning signs and promote timely appropriate corrective action (Part II).

Conduct effective reviews to verify that individual actions provide sufficient collective impact to achieve and sustain the desired outcomes (Part III).

Many people believe that the responsibility for leadership and review only apply to people at the top of the organization. However, leadership is a process, not a position in the hierarchy. No matter where you sit in the hierarchy, *everyone* is a top manager of something below. For this reason, *On Target* uses the term leader to denote every change agent at every level of enterprise who wishes to make something happen for dramatic effect. Anyone can direct, inspire, track, and partner with others to accomplish ambitious goals that stretch toward a vision. Everyone can experience the joy and fulfillment of successfully solving key leadership challenges.

If you have tried something and failed, or if you are not achieving your objectives fast enough, then read on to discover the power of review. Through a continual process of problem prediction, reflection, and timely corrective action, anyone can learn how to be professional and gain personal power by delivering commitments. You can then bask in the glow of achievement and recognition for rapid strategy implementation. Read on to discover how you *can* do it.

PART I

CHOOSE WHAT TO REVIEW

I RECENTLY ASKED the middle manager of a property and casualty insurance company if she agreed with the strategic plan for her company. She looked thoughtful and replied, "Actually, I have no idea what it is. There are some product development teams working on some new policy structures, but my department is not involved. You should talk to the head of our division; he'll know more about the executive strategy. We prepare a claims analysis for him each year before the strategic planning off site. All the presentations go in a book; actually, it's two books this year, with all kinds of marketing data, competitive benchmarks, and policy performance. He'll have that book. He can tell you more about the long-term strategy."

"So, how do you know what are the critical success factors for your company?" I asked.

Promptly she replied, "That's simple. The executive team has told us to focus on customer satisfaction and continuous improvement. These priorities are displayed on the wall in the lobby in the vision statement and in all of our customer literature. All of us are supposed to identify improvement opportunities in our daily work and take responsible action. If we continually improve our operations, then over time we always will be better than our competitors."

"Given this vision, then what are *your* particular priorities for the year?" I asked.

"Ironically," she responded, "the problem is that *everything* is important. My boss gives me target objectives each year that his boss gives him. And then we have our department financial objectives to meet budget each month. And in our customer studies, we find other things we need to do to satisfy the customer. The reengineering team is setting new standards for us. And then, of course, things come up throughout the year. There are so many priorities these days that I and my colleagues sometimes feel discouraged. It seems that nothing is ever enough."

"How then do you know if you are doing a good job?" I asked.

She shrugged her shoulders and looked squarely into my eyes. "When I go to my annual review, I never know how I'm going to be measured. We don't seem to change in the industry ranking of top insurance companies. So the best that I can do is to keep my boss happy. By the time we get to my year-end review, the priorities have changed so many times that last year's targets usually aren't relevant any more."

A COMMON MISTAKE IS TO TACKLE TOO MANY THINGS

Sadly for this woman and her company, her leadership has lost the power of focus. Yielding to the incessant pressure for change, many leaders ask workers to search for any and all improvements in quality, cost, delivery, and speed. This continuous incremental improvement philosophy has become a de facto strategy for many companies.

The mistaken belief is that if everyone continues to work harder and smarter, then the company will assuredly achieve and maintain a market leadership position. However, numerous uncoordinated incremental changes only cause a loss of strategic focus. With the haphazard pursuit of many small changes here and there, the organization systematically devolves toward competitive homogeneity and vanilla vision statements. In the end, many leaders merely create a hyperactive, overstressed environment in which people are "chasing too many rabbits," and no one can verify contribution. This strategic confusion is evident in the large number of "priority" business measures.

In a complex business environment, no leader can watch all the people, all the activities, all the warning signs, all the time. For this reason, wise leaders identify, monitor, and control the *few* opportunities that offer the *greatest* advantage to the organization and specify precisely how much is enough.

"Well," you might be thinking, "we cannot afford to pick just a *few* annual objectives. We have too many customers to serve, too many products to deliver, and too many inefficiencies. What are we supposed to do about the many other opportunities for operational excellence?" The answer is simple. Do what you have always done. But for rapid reliable results, pick only a few priority objectives and then rigorously review them throughout the year. If you cannot perform one thing well or reliably accomplish three things in one year, then you certainly cannot accomplish fifty-two things or even twelve.

TRACK THOSE THINGS THAT MATTER MOST TO THE ORGANIZATION

Choosing annual priorities is not easy. It takes wisdom, creativity, and courage to differentiate where we *could* improve, from where we *should* focus, from where we *must* focus, from where we *will* intervene. However, when you pick the right two or three priority objectives, they will naturally guide many other subordinate activities and measures. To this end, Part I shows how to sort through the many improvement opportunities competing for attention to select the most important items for continual review. Specifically, it will show how to

- identify the critical few annual objectives,
- assign and align individual responsibilities with these priority objectives, and
- control the calendar to deliver commitments on time.

These three focusing steps set the stage for change and provide the basis for continual review. Together, they ensure that daily activity focuses on those things that matter most to the organization.

CHAPTER 1

WHAT ARE THE CRITICAL SUCCESS FACTORS?

SELECT ANNUAL PRIORITIES

A life extended in a thousand directions risks depression and madness.

—May Sarton

A compelling vision and strategy set the stage for change. They can mobilize people with many different backgrounds to work toward a shared future. Yet they do not tell people what they must change in the next few months to reach the vision and how much is enough. A critical part of the leader's job is to identify and champion the few most important capabilities requiring intervention and continual review.

Annual objectives provide one tool to focus the organization in the short term. Whereas the vision states, "This is where we are going," annual goals state, "These are the vital few gaps or capabilities that we must close or acquire in the next fiscal year to reach our vision."

Vital and *few* are two key words. To be vital, an annual objective will describe a critical business parameter that *must change* to achieve the vision. To remain few, the leadership must make hard choices and difficult trade-offs to set *priorities*. Let's take a look at one leader's choice of annual objectives.

ANNUAL OBJECTIVES COMMUNICATE STRATEGIC PRIORITIES FOR THE FISCAL YEAR

Bob is the CEO of a national linen service company. His primarily regional organization is thriving, and he is pursuing an aggressive acquisition strategy. He has expended significant resources to train his executives and others in continuous quality improvement, root-cause problem-solving skills, customer focus, and process control. He is convinced that these management skills and philosophies will create a solid foundation for a healthy common culture in a growing company. Unfortunately, Bob is not getting the results that he desires. He sent me the annual plan depicted in Figure 1-1 for my review.

Bob believes in leadership focus. However, these annual objectives provide little guidance to his organization. His annual plan looks more like a statement of values than an annual plan. Among other things, it fails to

- show how these annual objectives will *drive* the long-term strategy,
- communicate the size and *difficulty* of the performance gaps, and
- clarify how he will measure and *track* progress.

These and other factors are critical to success. The more clear the priorities, the more easily everyone can focus on what really counts and take action.

FIGURE 1-1 Annual Objectives for Linen Service Company

People

Ensure That Management Is Focused on People

Service

All Service Deliveries Will Be Complete

Ensure That the Replacement of Worn Items Are Completed in a Timely Manner

Service Departments Will Be Better Trained

Profits

Strengthen the Management Team

Define a Strategy to Improve Weak Companies

Growth

Confidential

PLANNING IS A FOCUSING PROCESS

Most people naturally assume that their leaders know where they are going and that every annual objective supports the strategic intent. Contrary to that popular belief, many personnel are pursuing annual goals with little or no known strategic value.

Many leaders lack a clear understanding of which core competencies will create a competitive difference. These same leaders often mask their uncertainty with broad declarations like "go public," "be customer focused," "make three billion dollars in revenue," or "be the leader in the industry." But what do these statements really mean? What precisely must people accomplish in the next year to ensure such favorable outcomes? And how can they verify strategic progress? Declarations alone provide little behavioral guidance. They do not create a customer, nor do they show how to create future value.

Lacking direction, many leaders focus on the short-term financial needs of the enterprise. Year after year, they select annual goals to meet an operating budget, one that is often disconnected from, even finalized *prior* to, the strategic plan. Even more disconcerting, financial measures typically describe lagging outcomes. They track the "whats," not the "hows." So, from year to year, lacking tactical information, as annual goals are over- or underachieved, the leadership naively starts over again with new goals and objectives hoping they might again make inroads toward the vision.

IDENTIFY THE CRITICAL FEW SUCCESS FACTORS

"Well," you might be thinking, "I am sure that my leaders have a clever strategy. They fully understand the competitive challenges in our industry, and they routinely conduct strategic planning meetings. I am sure that our annual objectives support the strategic intent." Many people believe that if they have not seen or heard the strategy, then it must be a brilliant secret strategy, too sensitive to share for fear that someone will inform competitors. Ironically, many strategic plans marked "confidential" provide much to read but little guidance or direction.

This was evident in the detailed strategic plan that I recently reviewed for a large interconnect company. The business plan "summary," over twenty pages long, began with a generic vision statement to "shape the future" and "provide value and opportunity"; then followed with an industry-typical mission statement; a list of sixteen strategic objectives, including financial goals for market share, sales growth, return on equity, and the words "to be the recognized leader and benchmark for future technologies and capabilities" and "expand key supply chain partnerships"; seven "strategic-opportunity" options; eight "strategic fit" objectives, including "add to management depth and talent base" and "expand core competencies"; eight directives to develop detailed business plans; and seven "next steps", including "continue to make Q4 happen every quarter" and "create a new three-year strategic plan."

Now, just how confused are *you*? A company like this does not need to mark its strategic plan "confidential" because it doesn't tell a competitor anything, except that it's out of control. It provides no clear direction, no clear priorities, no critical path, and no quantitative measures to track progress. Nowhere in the "summary" pages does it articulate a few clear policies to guide daily activities, decisions, and resource allocations throughout the year.

SIMPLIFY THE MESSAGE

While facts inform every plan, data analysis is *not* the objective of the strategic planning process. Rather, the purpose is to reach consensus on which critical few structural attributes must *change* to thrive in the new environment. This ideal state or new way of operating is called a *vision*. The stated business purpose is called a *mission*. The fundamental beliefs that will not be compromised for financial gain are called *values*. The set of new capabilities that change the rules of the game for competitive advantage is called a *strategy*. And the core competencies needed to materialize the strategy in the next fiscal year are called *annual objectives*.

Some people incorrectly assume that a vision is based on pie-in-the-sky abstract imaginations. But a compelling vision describes the ideal organization we wish we had today based on factual evidence of trends and developments. The most powerful annual objectives attack the factual root barriers to this vision and build the core competencies needed to transform ourselves into what we need to be in the future.

ISOLATE THE RADICAL NEW REQUIREMENTS

Annual objectives bridge the gap between how we function now and how we need to behave to realize our vision. Not surprisingly, this vision gap is often quite large.

Many people get scared when they encounter a dramatic vision gap. These same people often select annual objectives that reflect what they *can* do today. Phrases like "We don't have the resources" or "We lack access to those distribution channels" provide easy excuses to propose incremental strategies and modest improvements and often masquarade as "realistic," "10 percent per year" plans.

Incrementally improving what we already know how to do is not an adequate strategy in today's turbulent environment. There are some things that we simply *must* accomplish even if we lack the capability today. To ensure the continued health of the organization, we must shift from a focus on mere *improvement* to focus on *transformation.* Consider the following illustration.

In *Chicken Run,* a recent animated film, a group of plucky chickens happily produce eggs until they discover that the grumpy hunchback chicken farmer and his greedy wife no longer value their egg-producing capabilities and purchase an evil machine that turns chickens into pies. Realizing they must escape, the chickens concentrate effort at passing the barnyard fence that once defined home and now confines them to a death camp. While maintaining satisfactory levels of daily egg production, they unsuccessfully attempt to jump, flap, burrow, and catapult themselves to freedom only to conclude that they must all escape on a flying machine, a technical capability they lack. Undaunted, they collaborate to apply latent skills and talents to prove the impossible—that, after all, chickens *can* fly, much to the bewilderment of the defeated farmer and his nasty wife.

As the chickens in this barnyard parable learned, to survive and thrive in a changing environment, we must continually plan and track two kinds of activity:

- Daily management activity maintains and *incrementally improves* the stability, predictability, and reliability of the *current* system. This activity improves procedural or operational effectiveness, *how* routine activities are performed to satisfy current customer requirements. These day-to-day processes, *or business fundamentals*, are well understood, and the organizational structure is already in place. In the barnyard story, the chickens perfect their routine skills of egg production to maintain the health of the existing barnyard business.
- Breakthrough activity *dramatically changes* the system structure to acquire what radical *new* capabilities must be acquired to create *future* value. This strategic activity changes the direction of the organization and the rules of the game by *redefining* the criteria for success. Often, the solution is unknown and requires an

entirely new process, a radical new resource allocation, and cross-functional collaboration. These stretch challenges are often called *breakthrough objectives*. In the barnyard story, apart from routine egg production, the chickens focus collective energy on acquiring a radical new capability, flight.

To remain healthy, we must continue to incrementally improve the business fundamentals that maintain current customer satisfaction *and* achieve the breakthroughs that alter the direction of the enterprise for future success. Figure 1-2 illustrates the need for both activities in the pursuit of excellence.

USE BACKWARD PLANNING TO CHART THE CRITICAL PATH

Strategic breakthroughs often require concentrated effort over an extended time frame, beyond one planning cycle. To chart the critical path, wise leaders identify and sequence the vital few drivers that will leap frog toward the vision. They translate the generalities of the vision and long-term plan into a sequence of measurable stretch objectives that everyone can collectively act on in the short term, often twelve months.

This is not a forward-planning process. Rather, the leaders work backward from a fact-based compelling vision to identify and sequence the nonfinancial root barriers to success. First, they study the vision gap to identify all the limiting factors. Then, they skim all incremental opportunities from the strategic plan and assign them to daily management. Next, they rank the remaining breakthrough candidates by degree of difficulty, strategic impact, customer focus,

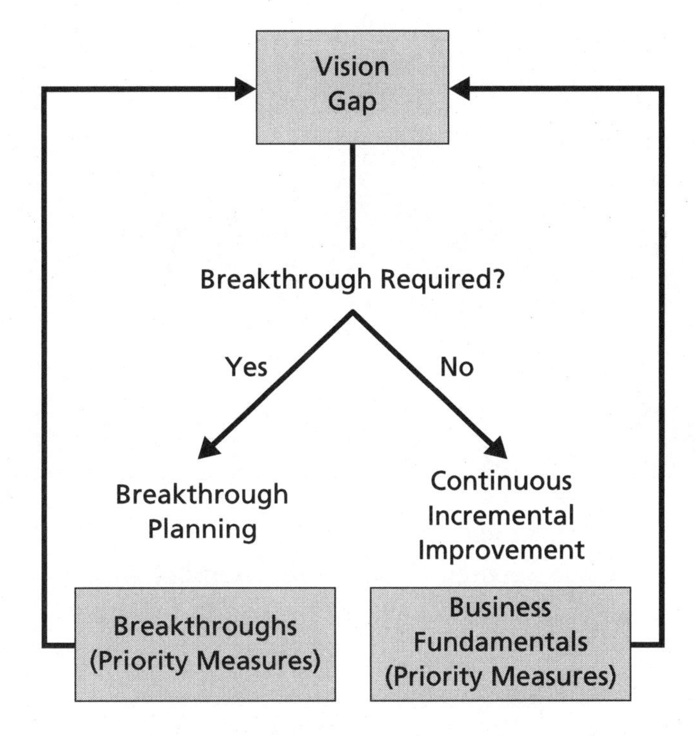

FIGURE 1-2 Two Kinds of Activity Close a Vision Gap

and timing. Finally, they lay the breakthrough challenges out in reverse. The result is a breakthrough map for *undoing* the current system.

A root barrier planning process is not difficult. Rather, it follows a few common sense planning principles:

- Select the objectives *prior* to the budgeting process.
- At every stage, focus on the *few* root barriers to progress.
- Let the size and difficulty of the breakthroughs dictate the *natural implementation time frame* even if beyond one planning cycle.

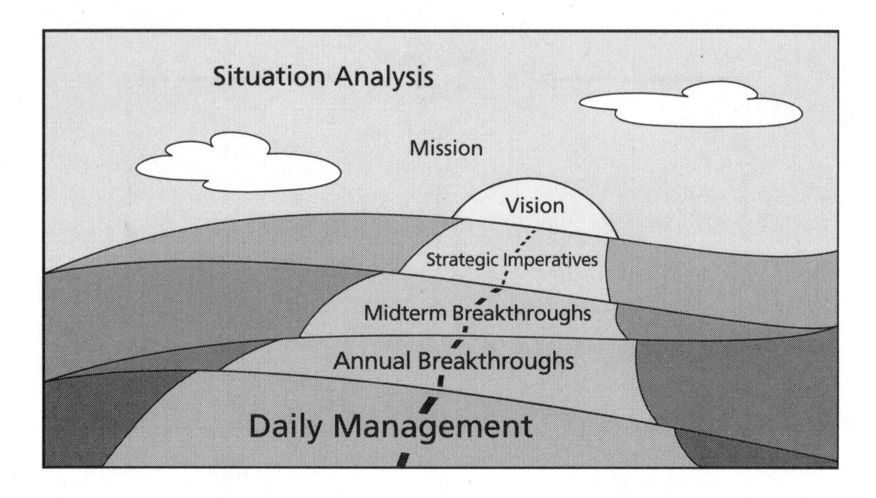

FIGURE 1-3 Chart the Critical Path
Source: Michele Bechtell, *The Management Compass* (Blackhall Publishing, Dublin, 1995).

- *Sequence* the breakthroughs such that annual objectives stretch toward the midterm breakthroughs and long-term strategy.
- Always translate words into *measures*.

Any opportunities not selected for breakthrough focus are managed through daily management using the tools and techniques for continuous incremental quality improvement.

TRACK TWO SETS OF ANNUAL PRIORITIES

This root barrier planning process is sometimes called *backward planning*, since this methodology works in reverse from the long-term vision to derive the mid- and short-term requirements: The mission, vision, and long-term plan drive the three- to five-year objectives ("If this is our vision and strategic plan, then what must we accomplish by three years from today?"). The midterm plan drives the annual objectives ("If this is where we must be in year 3, then what obstacles *must* we overcome within the next twelve months?"). Any opportunities not selected for breakthrough focus are ranked to select the priority parameters for daily management.

The result is a dual set of annual priorities:

- *Annual business fundamentals* describe the three to five priority measures of *routine* activity that require *incremental* improvement in the next twelve months. Business fundamentals are not a random list of business measures. Nor are they a list of all processes. They are a focused set of metrics requiring continuous incremental improvement of *known methods* in daily management.
- *Annual breakthroughs* describe the one to three vital few *dramatic* changes in system-level performance that can be accomplished in one year and will catapult the organization toward its midterm breakthroughs and long-term vision. Because these achievements typically require radical structural change and are strategically so significant, these stretch challenges are reviewed rigorously but separately throughout the year.

Over time, daily management and breakthrough activity work together. When we achieve a breakthrough in one planning cycle, we can standardize and incrementally improve the new methods through daily management to maintain the new levels of performance in subsequent cycles.

A BREAKTHROUGH PLAN CATAPULTS THE ENTERPRISE TOWARD ITS VISION

A root barrier, or backward, planning process provides a systematic approach to innovative redesign. It avoids straight, linear predictions of change, an inappropriate approach to innovation. And the plan is usually shorter than the typical ten-year linear plan. Because breakthrough challenges are often interrelated, the focus is on synergy and impact.

This marks one key difference between a breakthrough plan and an extensive set of aligned strategic measures. A breakthrough plan is a set of *measurable sequenced priority objectives* organized by size, difficulty, and timing. It charts the *critical path* (e.g., the few most important success factors). It isolates the few breakthroughs from other more modest improvement opportunities. Powerful features include focus, linkage, and clear measures of success.

What exactly does a critical path or breakthrough plan look like? Breakthroughs define the strategic imperatives no matter how many or few people are required. They communicate the one to three stretch capabilities, different from rivals, that will dramatically change the basis of competition. The critical path summarizes and links the measurable root barriers to progress that, when eliminated, will leapfrog the enterprise toward it's vision.

Many people worry that they will pick the wrong objective or mistakenly believe that their industry is too volatile to commit to a particular strategic breakthrough. Yet, even in a turbulent environment, nontrivial structural changes are at work. Think out over the next several years, imagine the ideal organization you wish you had today, and ask, "What is our unique interpretation of the critical success factors to achieve our vision?" and "Which business parameters will retain crucial importance three to five years from now?" Here are three examples of midterm breakthroughs:

- Reduce the number of parts needed in its cars by 30 percent in three to five years. (Nissan Motor Company)
- Achieve 100 percent on-time delivery for all products in three years. (AT&T Network Systems)
- Reduce quality returns as a percentage of revenue to less than 0.1 percent in three years. (Texas Instruments Semiconductor Group)

Each of these midterm objectives describes a perceived strategic, high leverage point that the leadership believes will change the rules of the game for dramatic advantage.

By definition, every midterm breakthrough will require supporting annual breakthroughs within the extended planning horizon. For example, a midterm breakthrough for a domestic company such as "Increase worldwide market share to 50 percent in three years" might require several annual breakthroughs, such as these:

- Year 1: Reduce new product development cycle to less than 120 days.
- Year 2: Penetrate Asian market for 20 percent market share.
- Year 3: Convert three major European OEMs (Original Equipment Manufacturers).

The hardest part of selecting annual priorities is to accept and live with the choices you make. A decision to focus on one or two aspects of your business is also a decision to give up other opportunities. This does not mean that business will not proceed as usual with its routine and pressing concerns. Rather, we must carefully manage our calendar to accomplish the critical few tasks needed to achieve our priorities. To make the final selection, it can help to ask, "What if we select this challenge?" "What if we don't?" and "Will this accomplishment remain critical despite daily distractions throughout the year?" Annual objectives focus attention, energy, and resources on the few goals that offer dramatic advantage to the organization.

CONVERT WORDS INTO MEASURES

Some leadership teams can get away with simple words and phrases to communicate and track their priorities. However, the ambiguity of language often creates variable interpretations of success and disappointing results. This can be especially troubling in a large or worldwide company requiring activity across many organizations, geographic regions, and spoken languages. Even within a small company, the manufacturing, finance, legal, and marketing languages can prevent a shared understanding.

To reduce the potential for misunderstanding, wise leaders use a vital few *measures* to summarize and make visible the master plan. To translate the words into measures, some of these leaders use the "five-element" rule: They state the directional (1) *objective* such as "Reduce late deliveries." Then they assign a (2) *unit measure* of success such as a count or ratio, a (3) *target value* to indicate the size of the gap, a (4) *deadline*, and the single (5) *owner* who will be accountable for closing the gap. Some people question whether every objective can be measured in quantita-

BOX: Many Annual Objectives Fail Right from the Start

- They are too numerous to remember.
- They lack a clear measure of success.
- They fail to drive the long-term strategy.
- They fail to specify the size or difficulty of the performance gap.
- They require an extended planning horizon beyond the annual cycle.
- They lack linkage over time.
- They do not derive from a factual gap analysis.

tive terms. The answer is yes. Every goal and objective can be translated into a vital few measures of success by asking these questions: How will I know when I accomplish this objective? What should get better? How will I measure that? The metric answers to these questions clarify direction and motivate action.

Strategy control measures can be easily displayed in a one-page diagram. Sometimes called the "CEO's framework," these priority metrics

- simplify the plan,
- communicate the critical path success factors,
- show the factual gaps requiring disciplined review,
- summarize the cause, and, effect relationships that will drive results,
- enable everyone to track progress the same way, and
- provide tangible evidence that change has occurred.

The CEO's framework is not an exhaustive list of measures. Rather, with a *few* words and numbers, it organizes and displays the logical relationships among the annual, midterm, and long-term priority objectives to articulate the leadership's theory for business success.

BOX: Qualities of Annual Breakthroughs

Annual breakthroughs

- focus on the customer;
- change the basis of competition;
- describe a stretch challenge;
- require a radical new allocation of resources;
- appear to be "undoable";
- describe a behavioral change in methods;
- require a year-long effort; and
- are few in number, no more than three.

SUMMARY

Annual objectives communicate the critical path for change. They identify the most promising tangible accomplishments that everyone can understand and act on in the next twelve months. The most effective annual objectives are strategic, measurable, and few in number.

So how can we direct the organization to focus on these annual priorities? How can we assign our talented people and allocate scarce resources to accomplish these priority goals? Many leaders gamble on the capability and good intentions of people to run with the flag. These same leaders later lack the means to verify that local strategies are sufficient to achieve the annual plan. This leads us to the next chapter, where we learn how to assign and align individual roles and responsibilities for maximum impact and continual review.

CHAPTER 2

WHAT IS MY ROLE?

ASSIGN AND ALIGN INDIVIDUAL CONTRIBUTIONS

As one of our counselors pointed out, it was an annual dream, not an annual plan.

—Ron McCormick

The best-laid plans leave nothing to chance. Unfortunately, too few leaders take this seriously. When asked, "How did you intend to achieve your annual plan?" many leaders answer, "By asking everyone to interpret the priorities and do their best." These same leaders wonder why, when they flip the switch at the top of the organization, the lights don't go on below.

Numerous factors can cause a breakdown in circuitry so that the "lights don't go on." Key players can misinterpret visionary language or develop incompatible plans. Capabilities may not match commitments. And personnel changes may disrupt continuity. These and other complications reduce effectiveness in achieving any goal or objective.

To focus people on the annual imperatives, wise leaders create a detailed company-wide plan of attack. They take the time to align individual activity with those things that matter most to the organization.

They ask important questions such as "What needs to change?" "Who needs to work together?" "Do they feel committed to the overall plan?" "What does each person need to contribute?" "How will we track progress?" and "Do individual plans add up to meet our annual objectives and close strategic gaps?"

CREATE A COMPANY-WIDE PLAN OF ATTACK

"Well," you might be thinking, "we already assign individual goals and objectives. These are determined between boss and subordinate." While some leaders do cascade annual objectives downward in the organization, they do so in a way that creates error and wastes valuable resources. Consider the following example.

Don is the CEO of a software design services company. Frustrated that his company was not progressing fast enough to meet investor expectations on Wall Street, he asked for my evaluation of the annual objectives he negotiated with each member of his executive team. This is what I found:

- The senior vice president of marketing described an innovative concept for two new promotions: a booth at the annual industry trade show and the integration of all marketing literature to reflect a single corporate image.
- The information systems department submitted a ten-page matrix of personnel assigned to tasks too numerous to list in this chapter, with a detailed project plan showing resource consumption by the fifty-two weeks of the fiscal year.
- The annual targets for the vice president of sales included a set of aggressive revenue

targets and a hiring plan for the addition of two new sales reps.

- The customer service department committed to several ambitious measurable goals to reduce complaint handling time and increase on-time deliveries.
- The human resource department submitted a list of seven action items including company-wide training in leadership and time management, developing an orientation program for new hires, and administering a morale survey to minimize attrition rates.

This variable set of goals was just the tip of the iceberg in a haphazard collection of planned activities and contributions. By function, level, and geography, individual goals varied in length, style, and format. Among the many lists of paper commitments, nowhere could I find clear measures of success, a clear strategic linkage, or the means to verify collective impact or track interim progress. Contrary to his good intentions, this CEO had created an environment of strategic impotence and learned helplessness.

MANY LEADERS CANNOT VERIFY COLLECTIVE IMPACT

"How did you and your people select these goals?" I asked Don.

He responded thoughtfully, "I asked each executive to review the three-year financial plan, vision, and annual breakthroughs. Then I asked them to propose a set of aggressive goals to achieve the plan. I reviewed their goals one-on-one in a private meeting with each of them. I gave them feedback on their performance on last year's goals, and then I added any goals that I felt should be on their plan. We've had two personnel changes on the executive team this year, so I was starting from scratch with two of my people. That took some extra time because their management styles are different from the two people who left the company. I made minor changes on most of the plans. But some of the sales goals were not aggressive enough. I raised those targets over the objections of the VP of sales to motivate the sales force to achieve some dramatic improvement. It's the dance we go though every year."

"How do people know what everyone else is working on?" I asked.

"I held a group meeting so that everyone could see everyone else's goals," Don replied. "That was an uncomfortable meeting. It seems like everyone thinks they're being asked to do more than the next guy to shoulder the burden of the financial plan. So I finally ended the meeting and just told them that there would be no more discussion. We just *have* to make plan. And they just have to work together!"

"What about the rest of the organization?" I asked. "How do they develop their annual targets?"

Don responded casually. "Like most companies, I guess, that's the responsibility of each executive," he said. "They assign individual annual goals when they conduct performance reviews with their personnel. Each manager has his or her own style. Some managers assign quality improvement teams to key challenges. Others assign individual objectives to their subordinates. The human resource department helps in that process."

"So, how do you know whether all the goals and objectives are sufficient to meet plan?" I asked.

"I don't know," he replied. "That's what I need you to tell me." He smiled and took a phone call.

Like Don, many leaders assign individual objectives in the hopes of motivating people to focus on the most important factors for success. Yet, they never reap the full benefits of strategy deployment. Too often,

- leaders plan for other people,
- people "chase too many rabbits,"
- individual objectives become disconnected from the strategy, and
- leaders fail to verify collective impact.

These and other limitations of traditional cascading methodologies often produce disappointing outcomes. Let's take a look at some helpful alignment protocols.

INVITE THE PEOPLE RESPONSIBLE FOR IMPLEMENTING THE PLAN TO INFORM THE PLAN

Some people, like Don, simply "know" what others should do to close vital gaps. So they busy themselves with enforcing preconceived tactics. These individuals often waste much time and energy to little effect. In the absence of shared commitment, they later feel the need to nag, lecture, punish, coerce, scold, plead, threaten, and/or reward to achieve their desired results. In the end, the question remains "Who is controlling whom?" We cannot control people; they make their own commitments.

At the other extreme, some leaders create an environment of learned helplessness where individuals lack a personal connection to the factual collective business results. This often happens when leaders treat top-level strategies as confidential: Only an elite group is privy to critical information. And power is measured by the extent to which an individual has access to closely held information. These same leaders wonder why people at the boundary of the organization often pursue strategies several years out-of-date.

Rapid strategy deployment requires rapid knowledge exchange. For this reason, wise leaders share the strategic challenges and logic behind their choices with everyone who possesses knowledge of a possible solution. Then they invite the people on whom the annual plan depends to design the plan. They understand that people choose to change themselves. So they ask the people closest to the realities of the business system to study the desired outcomes (the "whats") and identify the key strategies (the "hows"). The result is an aggressive, creative, coordinated plan based on the real capability of the organization.

FOLLOW A SYSTEMATIC DEPLOYMENT PROCESS

A key principle of rapid strategy deployment is explicit vertical and horizontal linkage. When cause and effect are loosely coupled, individual activity becomes a matter of trial and error. Such a haphazard approach to achieving business objectives is neither reliable nor repeatable.

"Well," you might be thinking, "we already cascade objectives. What is so different here?" An effective deployment systematically links key business objectives to all the necessary people in the organization in a way that everyone can see the big picture. What does this look like? Level by level, leaders communicate the why, what, when, and how much is needed, but not the how. Rather, employees use facts and causal analysis to design plans based on the true capability of the organization. Then they assign simple measures to track and verify collective impact.

Called "catchball," this disciplined fact-based participatory planning process encourages people to vertically and horizontally "toss back and forth" the practical details such as who, what, when, how, and how much to create a realistic yet ambitious plan. Catchball follows a three-step process:

1. Cascade the direction.
2. Negotiate individual contributions.
3. Roll up the plans to verify impact.

You achieve vertical alignment on the way down and horizontal alignment on the way up. A fact-based dialogue continues until everyone understands, agrees, and commits to the essence and urgency of the plan. The process is complete when senior leaders can verify that individual contributions collectively deliver the vital few annual requirements. The final set of linked individual quantitative contributions form the management "contract" between each level of the hierarchy.

CASCADE THE BIG PICTURE

A successful deployment begins with a description of the big picture. But, this is not a one-way communication. Starting at the top, level by level, the leadership builds the case and provides the rationale for the vision, the strategic imperatives, and the priority measures of success. They define new or key vocabulary, identify new areas of increased knowledge, and provide the facts behind their strategic choices. Again, the emphasis is on the what, not the how.

The prevailing question during the cascading process is "Are leaders articulating the plan in a way that is clear?" It may initially seem perfectly obvious to the senior leadership. Yet someone may ask, "Why are you looking for a 20 percent reduction in cost?" Is that realistic given where we are this year"? Or "Do you mean 20 percent across the board"? A fact-based dialogue continues until everyone understands and commits to the basic plan, the factual choice of the targets and the methods, and the factual degree of urgency.

A compelling story helps leaders communicate strategies in three ways: It enables stakeholders to discover a personal relationship to the corporate objectives enhancing commitment and alignment. It expands the horizon of awareness to unleash creative forces and link local problems with the strategic objectives. And it provides a mental model to make sense of new information, retain it longer, and improve coordination.

USE CAUSAL ANALYSIS TO SELECT AND LINK INDIVIDUAL CONTRIBUTIONS

Many leaders fret that employee input will be uninformed, antagonistic, obstinate, or demanding. But when people are given a reliable set of rules and methods to select their strategies, operational knowledge always improves the quality of plans. The instruction is simple: "This is what I need, and this is the *alignment process* that I want you to use to select your supporting contributions."

Merely stratifying the outcome measure, breaking it down into smaller subsets, does not adequately define a supporting contribution. For example, cascading a target such as "reduce cost by 20 percent" fails to specify or control the how. As actions roll down the organization, the methods and strategies may change, yet the metrics do not (e.g., "reduce cost at the company level," "reduce cost at the division level," "reduce cost at the department level.") Outcome measures alone provide little guidance throughout the year and create a useless tracking system. We achieve greater control when we identify and monitor the supporting strategies.

To identify and control the performance drivers, wise leaders require that subordinates demonstrate the *logic* that will drive the results. They ask each person to make visible the cause-and-effect relationships between their proposed contributions (the hows) and the company annual objectives (the whats). Then they ask them to quantify the impact. Essential ground rules for choosing individual contributions include the following:

- *Clarify the objective.* "*What* is my superior's objective, and how is it being measured?"
- *Quantify the target level of performance.* "What is the factual *gap*, and how much is enough?"
- *Identify the root barriers to progress.* "*Why* is there a performance gap?"
- *Pick the vital few strategies.* "*How* will I close the gap? What one to three system changes will permanently eliminate the root barriers?"
- *Assign a measure of success to each strategy.* "What will we *track*?"
- *Verify that collective strategies will close the gap.* "What is the total quantitative *impact*, and will we meet our target?"

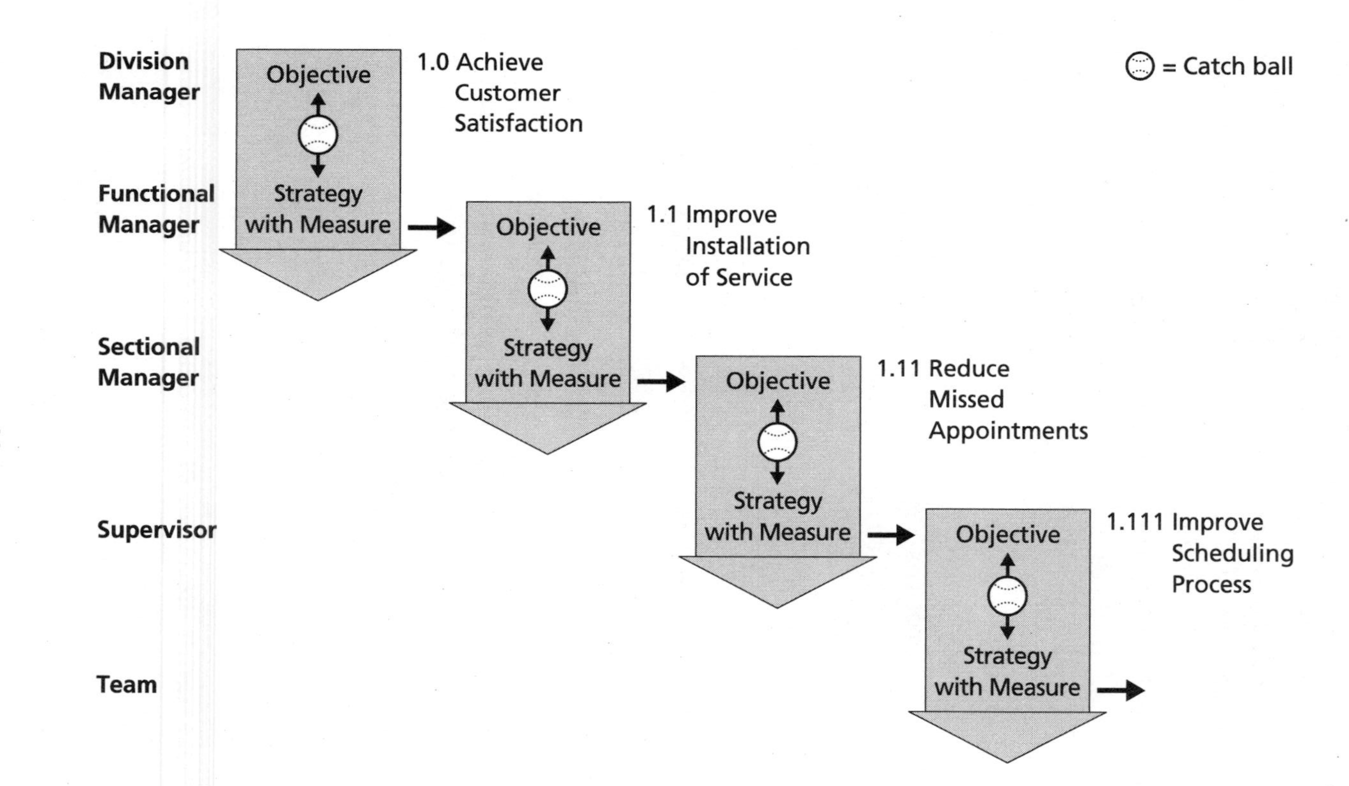

FIGURE 2–1 Rapid Strategy Deployment Requires Vertical Linkage of Means and Measures

This set of rules is variously called a *root-cause problem-solving process, causal analysis,* or *gap analysis.*

Such a systematic, fact-based planning process minimizes misalignments. Too often, individuals misuse annual objectives to justify pet projects. They attempt to link their project with an annual objective to gain significance. Anyone who disagrees with the project is subsequently accused of not being committed to the annual objective. Although there may be unwritten rules about how to resolve such disagreements, typically nothing exists in the structure of the planning process to resolve the situation. Little or no dialogue takes place about how the project *factually* supports the annual objective. And there is even less discussion as to whether the project is the *best* strategy to achieve the annual objective.

A cause-and-effect planning structure discourages individuals from darting off in many directions all in the name of the same annual objective or pursuing efforts that oppose one another. A systematic fact-based planning process ensures that the strategic intent is the focus of every local plan and that individual plans add up to deliver the strategic requirements. And it avoids the discontinuities in direction commonly experienced in the wake of personnel changes. Because all supporting strategies derive from a factual root cause gap analysis, a new participant can pick up where a prior owner left off with little or no loss in pace. Figure 2-1 illustrates the relationship between objectives and supporting strategies in a deployment plan.

ASSIGN MEASURES TO TRACK IMPLEMENTATION AND VERIFY IMPACT

The unit of measure for a supporting strategy is usually *different* from that of the objective because it describes a process parameter, or *leading* indicator, to drive the measurable objective. When you achieve a goal, you are actually experiencing the outcome of a sequence of reliable cause-and-effect actions. The process is similar to baking a cake. When we control the ingredients, temperature, and baking time (strategy control measures), then we increase the probability that we produce a moist cake (desired outcome measure).

Process control measures provide a reliable mechanism to track interim factual progress, for we can now track two things:

- *Are we implementing our strategies?* This can be determined by tracking the strategy control measures.
- *Did our strategies work*? This can be determined by tracking the outcome measures.

The deployment principle is simple: Control the methods and measures to control the outcome. When the methods, measures, and outcomes are linked, you don't just get results—you get *planned* results. A fact-based, systematic, alignment process defines the necessary leading process measures to guide the transformation. Linking the objectives with strategies enables everyone to work together to modify the system in real time.

Some project-oriented people initially propose milestones or deadlines to define a measurable contribution. However, *dates are not measures of success.* Deadlines suggest deliverables, activities, and busyness such as documentation, research, scheduled events, tasks, projects, and reports. Busywork never measures the success of our efforts. Rather, project deadlines such as "Install a computer system by end of third quarter" or "Conduct a sales promotion in the second quarter" describe an implementation schedule. And an implementation schedule is about project management, not quantitative changes in system performance. To convert any project into a measurable system level of improvement, ask "Why am I doing this?" "How will I measure success?" "How will I know that this project helped the organization?" These questions help identify key business parameters that will change.

MAKE VISIBLE THE LINKAGE

Another key principle for achieving rapid results is to track only a few priorities at every level of the hierarchy. So, wise leaders use a consolidating protocol to minimize the number of descending priorities. Called the *umbrella method,* one focusing methodology encourages people to view descending objectives as causes of some larger problem by asking, "What do these objectives have in common?" The answer will often suggest a single objective at a higher level of abstraction that will support the descending objectives.

Several other techniques can prevent descending objectives from growing too quickly. At a simple level, some leaders insist that no person commits to more than three objectives and no more than three strategies per objective. Whatever the ground rules, the purpose of strategy deployment is to link down, get focused, and control the impact.

A *tree diagram* provides one visual tool to display the vertical and horizontal linkage of the total plan. This "auditable" deployment plan has the following features:

- A structured hierarchical "tree of contribution" shows *explicitly* how objectives and strategies cascade down through the organization. The strategies, specific to each level of the organization, state what that level has to do to achieve the annual objective.

- A table of *control measures* provides the instrumentation to track whether each supporting strategy is being implemented and whether the strategies produce the desired impact.
- A *vertical numbering system* brings order and flexibility to the planning process. In response to new developments, one can surgically add, modify, or remove strategies, measures, targets, or owners to control the pace.

Not all supporting strategies are linear. Some achievements may attack root barriers to more than one high-level objective. The deployment plan or matrix must reflect these interrelationships. Whatever the form, the key is to display the causal relationships among the midterm breakthroughs, the annual breakthroughs, and the department objectives. All objectives are expressed in measurable terms using the five-element rule.

ROLL UP THE COMMITMENTS TO VERIFY CAPABILITY

In many companies, the planning process stops when objectives are cascaded to the lowest level of the organization. The belief is "Now that you know what we want, go do it."

For rapid strategy deployment, the planning process is only half over when objectives and means are cascaded from top to bottom. When the critical success factors have been translated into local contributions, a second process begins that is called the *roll-up process*. The roll-up process adds horizontal coordination to vertical integration. It provides bottom-up feedback to the leadership to communicate "Given our resource constraints, analysis, creativity, and experience, this is what we believe we can deliver."

The roll-up is essentially a capability check. Level by level, each manager reviews the individual plans below and across organizational boundaries to

- confirm deployment to the appropriate action levels,
- detect omissions and eliminate redundancies,
- settle conflicts or contradictions,
- reallocate resources for greater impact,
- assure vertical and horizontal alignment, and
- verify and strengthen collective impact.

The prevailing question during the roll-up phase is "If we implement all of these strategies, will we meet our goal?" The strategy deployment matrix of the vital few control measures provides the answer. If the answer is yes, then everyone can move directly to action.

DOCUMENT THE DUAL RESPONSIBILITIES

When all is said and done, what does an individual deployment plan look like? Like the high-level annual plan, deployment plans document and track two sets of responsibilities:

- the few stretch contributions that support the annual breakthroughs, and
- the priority incremental improvements for operational excellence.

Depending on the nature of the company's strategic breakthroughs, not everyone will significantly contribute to the achievement of these objectives. Yet, *every* person can improve the daily processes that keep the business healthy. Strategic breakthroughs often require detailed cascaded strategies to change the direction of the business. But, daily management priorities can usually be identified with a *decentralized* planning process, for the organization structure and process standards are already in place. Typically workers organize around the key processes that define a major functional area, such as production or marketing, and select the most important opportunities to reduce errors, duplication, and delays to enhance quality, cost, and delivery.

BOX: How Effective Are *Your* Contributions?

- *Consensus*—Do they reflect teamwork?
- *Focus*—Are they few in number?
- *Linkage*—Do they vertically support the strategy?
- *Method*—Did you use causal analysis to select a "how"?
- *Measure*—Does each "how" have a clear measure of success?
- *Transformation*—Did you specify breakthrough priorities and business fundamentals?
- *Impact*—Do these contributions quantitatively close the gap?

SUMMARY

"This alignment process is nice in theory," you might be thinking, "but we cannot afford to specify all the deployment details and verify linkage. It will take too much time and is too cumbersome." These are valid concerns. It does take time. And at times, it will feel tedious as teams debate and struggle to reach consensus on the essential means and measures to achieve strategic breakthroughs. But what happens if consensus is lacking among the people on whom you depend? What happens if individual contributions do not add up to close the gap? What happens if you lack measures to track interim progress? The answer is that you will fail to achieve your goals and objectives.

In the end, successful leaders do what unsuccessful leaders are unwilling to do. They use team planning, linkage, and measurement to assign and align roles and responsibilities. They demonstrate leadership and the courage to select the few priorities at each level of the organization. Yet, certain questions naturally follow: Once people know what to contribute and how to track progress, how should we spend our time? What are the most important tasks and calendar requirements to deliver our commitments? And how can we focus on these activities and avoid the common distractions of day-to-day business? This leads us to the next chapter, where we learn how to make the calendar work to achieve our individual commitments.

CHAPTER 3

HOW SHOULD I SPEND MY TIME?

DOCUMENT DEADLINES AND DELIVERABLES

Free time is made, not found, in the manager's job, by forcing it into the calendar.

—Henry Mintzberg

Take a look at your individual annual goals. Now, take a look at your calendar. How are you managing your time? What is the likelihood that you will meet your commitments? Will your planned calendar activities deliver the positive results that you want? How do you know?

Many people don't know. They schedule meetings with associates, customers, and suppliers, budget reviews, deadlines, and other busyness that reflects their routine responsibilities and responses to continual weekly surprises. They believe that the calendar will figure itself out as the year rolls around. So, week by week, they focus on the short term, reacting their way through the rest of the year. Banking on past skill at crisis management, they skip from small urgency to small urgency, from month to month, assuming that in the end, they will meet their annual goals. That is, of course, if their senior leaders really hold them accountable in the end. And so the calendar goes on, once again.

Such a reactive approach to achieving annual goals rarely produces reliable outcomes. Weekly distractions and routine activities associated with the status quo receive more attention than the structural changes needed to meet our goals. We procrastinate, and the activities necessary to achieve our year-end commitments never get performed: We may fully *intend* to conduct these precise activities we know we need to do, yet we never seem to devote the necessary time.

CREATE AN IMPLEMENTATION PLAN

To make the most of the calendar, wise leaders create a detailed implementation plan and tie it to their daily calendar. Annual objectives communicate *which* priority measurable gaps must be closed. They do not provide the tactical piece of *how* we intend to change the business system to elevate the critical levels of performance. In contrast, implementation, or action, plans describe the tangible activities that bring annual commitments to life. They translate good intentions into the practical details and calendar activities that ensure appropriate structural change.

A detailed action plan answers key tactical questions such as "Which steps and actions are needed first to close the priority gaps?" "What activities can we do simultaneously?" "What precisely do we need to change to achieve our annual goals?" and "What are the interim deadlines?" The more accurately we anticipate, document, implement, and update the critical tasks for fundamental change, the more reliable the results. This is just good project management. Figure 3-1 illustrates some common implementation barriers.

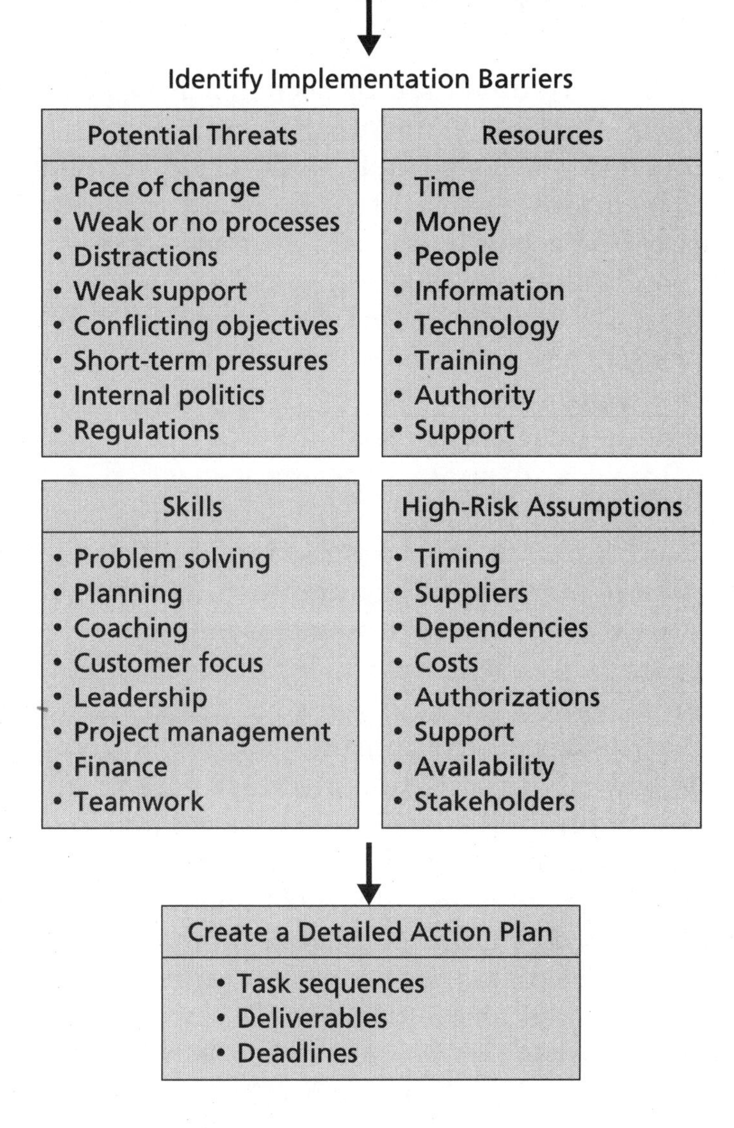

FIGURE 3-1 An Action Plan Translates Good Intention into Practical Details

Will My Changes Hold?

To develop an action plan, many people initially create a list of calendar activities, deliverables, or planned events. They assume that, by accomplishing each item on the list, they will eliminate their problem.

Simple "to do" lists rarely work. Once our changes begin to interact with other aspects of daily life, things often become more complicated. Actions invite reactions. Unintended side effects of early actions can increase the complexity of the problem. And, over time, people often drift back to old undesirable, high-risk behaviors causing the initial problem to return in an even more insidious way.

To make and sustain permanent change, wise leaders install new norms and procedures that will consistently deliver their desired results. They understand that significant change requires structural change. Consider the following story.

I recently met with Maria, a talented young engineer at a rapidly growing software design company. She was assigned the annual goal of reducing the costly gap between the number of requested changes in product specifications based on customer feedback and the number of actual changes evident on the product release date. Incomplete changes had been identified as a primary cause of product returns and customer dissatisfaction, two priority improvements identified at the company level. Inconsistent prerelease methods appeared to be the problem.

A new hire, Maria was committed to making a measurable difference and had worked nights and weekends to develop a training course for the software designers. The purpose of the seminar was to enlist their support by getting them to check the list of all requested changes before releasing the product.

This simple practice would reduce costly hours and budget overruns due to rework and product returns, and increase customer loyalty. Maria was enthustiastic about her action plan.

"What happens after the seminar"? I asked.

"I hope they will do all that I ask them to do," she replied. "They probably will, since they like me. I'm new, and the guy before me had a hostile relationship with them. When they see how important this is, then I believe they will review the check list." Maria was hopeful about her planned training.

"But what happens with new hires"? I asked.

"I plan to make a special meeting with any new people and go over the same stuff with them," Maria replied.

"And what happens if you get transferred?" I pursued. Maria looked discouraged. After all her enthusiasm, hard work, and planning, she saw that her training solution, while aimed at a fundamental cause of product returns, had built-in flaws. For all her efforts, her "solution" was vulnerable to predictable memory lapses, the goodwill of others, and personnel changes.

"All is not lost," I assured her. "Let's take a look at how you might use your planned time with the engineers to install a new step or protocol in the product release process, something that they can control to confirm adherence to recommended behavior."

Maria met with the software engineers later that month, not as a training seminar but as a problem-solving meeting. Over the next several months, with mutual support and joint agreement, the two departments analyzed the customer problem and added a "sign-off" step in the product release process. Today, Maria is the head of a branch sales office in another state. And many of the software engineers at the main office, new to this fast-growing company, have never met her. But, no software product leaves the company without the signature of the project manager, indicating that all change orders have indeed been satisfied. Maria and her team fixed the problem with a procedural change at the routine behavior level, and now everyone benefits, including the customer.

AVOID "HIT AND RUN" TACTICS

An action plan reveals our approach to the change process. A review of the action plan can answer: Are people analyzing the factual situation before making changes? Are people scheduling "quick fix" events, or are they making fundamental lasting changes in policies and procedures? Are people taking the review process seriously? These and other issues affect our likelihood of success.

Many people, like Maria, initially react to pressures for quick visible improvements with one-time solutions, event-oriented projects, or actions such as "run a promotion," "meet with the distributor," or "train everyone." They may even talk about implementing a "quality improvement program" or a "leadership training program." However, hit-and-run tactics, based on "A causes B, and that's that," promote an event mentality. They may mitigate a problem in the short term, but they fail to sustain progress over time.

Programs have beginnings and ends. How many change programs has your company attempted in the last ten years? Three? Five? Fifteen? More than twenty? It is not uncommon to hear that people lose interest after three to six months.

As Maria learned, significant change is not about temporarily managing *better* with programs, projects, or minor changes to business as usual. Rather, it is about managing *differently* by developing and standardizing new protocols and procedures designed for continuous improvement. An effective action plan designed for breakthrough requires a shift in focus from *improvement* to a focus on *transformation.*

This means that some things must come apart before new things can come together. To create an effective action plan for lasting change, wise leaders anticipate and manage the many interacting people, activities, resources, and time with as little disruption as possible. They tread softly to respect influential stakeholders and interrelationships. They refrain from scheduling reactive events to instead modify the protocols and behaviors that produce the desired level of performance. And they take the time to study the factual situation to identify, test, and verify the impact of their solutions. A systems thinker has a much better chance of accomplishing significant change than a systems tinkerer.

INSTALL A REPEATABLE PROCESS, NOT AN EVENT

As Maria learned, most disappointments derive from poorly designed processes. A *process* is any set of routine behaviors, steps, or activities that produce measurable outcomes. Inputs can include such things as supplies, information, and energy. Outputs can be anything from information in reports or data, to services or products. Problems derive from poor hand-offs, delays, and disconnects. And errors will linger until the process is changed.

To change the predictable outcomes, we need to change the predictable activities. For this reason, an effective action plan exhibits a process orientation rather than an event orientation. Process-oriented activities include documenting and mapping the process, analyzing unwanted variation, reaching consensus on a new process design, setting and controlling new standards, and assigning control measures to assess the effectiveness of the new process. The aim is to create and maintain new methods that meet and sustain the required performance to meet the annual objectives.

Unlike event mania, lasting change rarely yields an immediate high or instant gratification. Rather, it requires a careful systematic examination of the routine behaviors and cultural norms that keep us trapped at old dissatisfying levels of performance. And it requires discipline to alter these methods. This is the ultimate purpose of the action plan—to bring the system or key processes in line with the priority

BOX: Exercise 3-1: Does Your Calendar Speak Process Improvement?

Review your calendar from the past two weeks. Estimate how much time you spent in the following three categories. (The three combined should total 100 percent.)

Routine work (answering telephone messages, traveling, Internet, etc.) __________%

Firefighting (managing unhappy customers, employees, or suppliers) __________%

Improving processes (improving a billing system, improving the quality, delivery, or cost of internal activities for reliable results) to meet your annual objectives __________%

annual requirements to produce a factual level of proficiency that can be evaluated for reliability and effectiveness.

So, what does your distribution of time say about *your* commitment to process improvement as the means to achieve your annual objectives? Are you just talking about change, or are you making the structural changes to achieve it? Your calendar does the talking. Exercise 3-1 provides a simple self-test for determining the process orientation of your personal action plan and calendar activities.

RESPECT STAKEHOLDERS

Logic alone does not explain human or organizational behavior. As Maria discovered, numerous psychological and social issues—the "soft stuff"—such as employee morale, trust, workplace conditions, and the need for recognition can derail the most "obvious" solutions.

Many people initially ignore the fuzzy issues when they design their action plan. For them, only the rational aspects of the business such as performance metrics, task assignments, and reporting structures link cause and effect. These same people later bemoan coworker resistance to new ways and complain that their elegant strategies for improvement are not being implemented as intended.

To avoid complications and unnecessary delays, wise leaders ask diagnostic questions such as "What is the prevailing mood of those who work in the organization?" "What are their concerns, however irrational they may at first seem?" "Did we address the human issues in our tactics and strategies?" "Who else may be adversely affected by our 'solution'?" "How have we included them in the planning process and in the development of the solution?" More difficult to map, understand, and manage than the purely mechanistic aspects of the business, the soft issues often lead to failed objectives and delayed accomplishments. The more we invite key stakeholders to participate in the creative development of solutions, the more likely our changes will hold. An effective action plan shows sensitive attention to these affected parties.

Disappointing performance is often linked to a pattern of behavior over time. Seeing the pattern of behavior can often show us where we are trapped: "They always do *X*; we always do *Y*." To make significant change, we must often alter our own behavior. When we see a behavior pattern, we must then tell ourselves the truth by boldly answering the question "What exactly am I willing to do?" We must fix ourselves first by managing our predictable response.

MAKE VISIBLE THE LEARNING PROCESS

In the early stages of every problem-solving process, data are often scarce, and it is tempting to skip the facts and move right to action. But, anecdotal information alone can slow the change process.We must take the time to study the situation and factually verify the success of our proposed solutions.

At the heart of every change process is the scientific method for hypothesis testing. This is sometimes called the *plan-do-check-act* (PDCA) *cycle* for continuous improvement. To zero in on our targets, we plan our process improvements, do implement the structural changes, *check* the factual results on a frequent basis to diagnose which predictions did not come true, and *act* on our improved understanding of the business system. When we get the results that we want, we can then standardize the behaviors to create reliable results and sustain the gains.

Wise leaders design this experimental learning process into their action plan. They schedule activities to collect and analyze data, document and map processes, build consensus on new methods, and verify the effectiveness of strategies. Their action plans display activities related to each of the PDCA steps, especially the checking and acting phases. Frequent review and timely corrective action are critical to success.

USE A STANDARD ACTION PLAN TO DOCUMENT THE TACTICAL DETAILS

So how are you using *your* calendar? Does your implementation plan focus on improvement or transformation? Are you sending people to training courses or building skills through daily management? Are you conducting events or installing a reliable repeatable process? Are you pushing the change process or removing the root limiting factors? Are you reacting to unique situations or eliminating structural problems? Are you shifting the burden or changing your own behavior?

To evaluate proposed tactics, wise leaders standardize the implementation plan. They use a simple visual matrix to display the linkage among critical tasks and task sequences. They list the objectives, tasks, owners, and deliverables on the vertical axis and the monthly calendar with deadlines on the horizontal axis. Deliverables define the tangible evidence that an action item is complete to bring control to the change process. It is easier to evaluate the value and success of a "published report" than the activity "conduct research." Figure 3-2 illustrates an action plan from one company.

One visual tool, the tree diagram, can be used to identify and organize the critical tasks listed on the action plan. A team of people closest to the problem list the key implementation steps and place them on the first level of the tree diagram. For each major step, they ask "What could go wrong?" and add branches to the tree diagram to reflect the answers. Then for each identified problem, they list possible countermeasures in bubbles or clouds to suggest possible actions. They often use a symbol to denote their final selection of the most effective countermeasures, which are typically process changes. A tree diagram communicates the true complexity of a task and makes overwhelming tasks seem manageable.

The action plan is a rolling plan, and with practice, improves over time. Key success factors include:

- move deliverables and deadlines from the Action Plan to your daily calendar,
- put a review schedule in place,
- use the Action Plan to structure routine meetings,
- visually track progress on the action plan, and
- continually update the Action Plan.

Week in and week out, each of us utilizes precisely the same amount of time. The action plan is a tool for time management. It enables us to sustain focus on priority objectives despite daily distractions.

FIGURE 3–2 A Sample Action Plan

Objective: Improve the Management of our Inventory Owner: M. Martinez																
No.	Strategies	Action Items	Owner	Deliverables	1st Quarter			2nd Quarter			3rd Quarter			4th Quarter		
					Jan	Feb	Mar	Apr	May	Jun	Jul	Aug	Sep	Oct	Nov	Dec
1.1	Standardize and automate our order fulfillment process based on best practices.	**Standardize Codes**	P Lowe		S											
		Standardize Coding	P Lowe		S						E					
		Create Master List		Master list	S			E								
		Develop Data Collection Forms and Reports		Management approval			S				E					
		Develop Data Collection Entry Utility					S				E					
		Design Easy Paperwork		Focus group			S				E					

BOX: An Effective Action Plan Documents the Transformation

- Avoid "hit and run" tactics
- Respect stakeholders
- Make visible the learning process
- Outline the process improvements
- Document the deliverables and deadlines
- Assign a single owner to each deliverable
- Transfer deliverables to your daily calendar

SUMMARY

An action plan translates the good intentions behind annual commitments into structural change. It provides a vital tool to identify, sequence, and track the necessary accomplishments, responsible individuals, and deadlines for a speedy implementation. But, in a rapidly changing environment, it is difficult, if not impossible, to implement any plan as conceived. Initial assumptions and strategies often prove inadequate as events unfold. This leads us to Part II of this book where we explore the value of frequent review. The more quickly we can determine which strategies or tactics are failing and why, the more quickly we can take timely corrective action for rapid reliable results.

PART II

CONDUCT FREQUENT REVIEWS

I RECENTLY ASKED the vice president of a marketing services firm how often they reviewed their strategic objectives at the executive level.

"Quarterly," she replied.

"And how do you track progress in between?" I asked.

She looked a bit confused. "Every month we review our budget and financial goals at the department level," she responded.

"No, I mean, how do you know that your department is implementing its strategies fast enough to meet your annual company goals?"

She looked puzzled and then a little frustrated. "I'll find out at the quarterly review, and I ask periodically in the hallway."

I pressed on, "But wouldn't you like to know *now*, so you can determine where people are struggling and how to help them?"

Defensively, she replied, "I hire good people. They know what they are supposed to deliver, and I trust that they will. If they are behind on their commitments, they will let me know."

"But, how do you know that *they* know?" I persisted.

She picked up her papers and prepared to leave. "That's just the way we work at this company. There is no way to answer those kinds of questions."

Sadly for this executive and her company, these questions provide some of the highest leverage points that a leader can use to accelerate the rate of change and ensure reliable results. If you do not know precisely what you need to achieve this month to reach your annual commitments, then how can you promptly detect delays? If you do not know that you are off plan, then how can you study the situation to install timely corrective action? If you fail to install timely corrective action, then how can you test your "new and improved" assumptions and solutions before it is too late? How can you ever hope to reach your annual goals and objectives? You cannot. The more attentive the leader, the more reliable the results.

Many business leaders like this woman executive treat their annual goals and strategic plans as static. They agree to a set of annual measurable objectives, make initial calendar plans, and then look away. Perhaps one year later, they dust off their goals and reassess their relevancy. Lacking the wisdom that could be gained from past review, they begin again, often with new goals unrelated to prior ones.

Annual, even quarterly, strategy reviews provide *lagging* indicators of success. Leaders rarely catch deviations throughout the year and therefore rarely fix them. By taking too little action, too late, the leadership loses opportunity and flexibility to create a future of its own choosing.

To minimize error and accelerate change, wise leaders conduct frequent reviews of the strategic imperatives, at least monthly. They divide their annual commitments into twelve monthly increments and then rigorously track progress. These are not cursory financial reviews. Rather, they take the time to

- obtain factual evidence of change to detect early warning signs,

- analyze the gaps to identify the root limiting factors, and
- install timely countermeasures to control the transformation.

Some people worry that frequent review will drain precious time from other, more valuable activities. But what can be more important than tracking the critical few success factors? What is more pressing than implementing the structural changes that *must* occur to achieve a strategic position in the future? What is more valuable than the latest information on variance from the priority annual targets? Everyone needs a way to talk about business priorities in a way that keeps them alive and actionable. For this reason, wise leaders go beyond planning and doing to routinely check and act on the differences.

They use the monthly review to enhance the quality and speed of strategic action. Specifically they use three diagnostic questions to guide each monthly review.

- "Where are you off plan?"
- "Why are you off plan?" and
- "What corrective actions have you already taken to close the gap?"

Part II shows how these questions catapult people from inertia to action and sustain focus on priority objectives throughout the year. Factually reviewed on a frequent basis, they provide informed, provocative, self-motivating, and self-correcting action.

CHAPTER 4

WHERE AM I OFF PLAN?

TRACK DEVIATIONS FROM EXPECTATION

One accurate measurement is worth a thousand expert opinions.

—Grace Hopper

Timely failure information leads to success. The more quickly we can identify errors and delays such as incomplete plans, false assumptions, nonadherence to plan, and weak strategies, the more quickly we can focus leadership intervention for optimum impact.

Some people are afraid to admit failure or delays for fear of blame. They prefer *not to know* than to discover or confirm the truth of error. But this only creates a culture of self-denial and learned helplessness.

Willful ignorance is evident in the structure of many progress reviews. Many review meetings waste valuable time emphasizing where managers are *on plan*. Problems, when detected, remain poorly investigated. False assumptions become anecdotes. The quantitative impact of early failure goes undetermined. And naive actions create further unintended side effects.

ELICIT EARLY FAILURE INFORMATION

To identify and eliminate root impediments to progress, wise leaders build protocols and procedures to elicit negative information rapidly. They see management time as a precious resource for solving the most pressing problems of the business. And they see *failure* information as leading-edge information to find a way to make things work. So they routinely identify and study the predictions that did not come true.

In short, they track deviations from expectation. They dispense with presentations of where they are on plan, to focus *only* on where and why they are *off* plan. They replace passive presentations with an active problem-solving meeting that analyzes critical deviations for timely corrective action.

A deviation can be positive (ahead of schedule) or negative (behind schedule). Although most leaders initially concern themselves with negative deficiencies, any deviation from plan can create problems for others elsewhere in the organization. Deviations can include performance, magnitude of resources, and schedule.

Positive and negative deviations demand equal attention. This is because every deviation provides a valuable opportunity to uncover the assumptions that caused faulty predictions. Even when we achieve our desired results, it is important to verify that we achieved our results *because* of our plan. The purpose of a plan is to get *planned* results.

Some people initially believe that exposing failures will depress and discourage people. Contrary to popular belief, frequent review of factual deviations can turn traditional, boring, sleepy meetings into energized problem-solving forums, especially when the delays or failures impact critical business objectives. A monthly review of deviations

- keeps attention focused on the critical success factors,
- shows whether we are doing what we said we would do,
- shows whether our strategies are working, and
- provides factual evidence of change.

Problems become opportunities, not skeletons to be buried.

TRACK FACTUAL PROGRESS ON THE STRATEGIES AND OUTCOMES

"Well," you might be thinking. "we routinely submit progress reports. We review our action items and report any unusual problems or delays. What's so different here?" One answer is *factual* progress. Many people report on their "busyness" but fail to quantify the impact of their actions on goals. They informally chat with others in the hallway, share anecdotal problems, and communicate changes in direction.

Informal updates provide colorful stories and suggest opportunities for leadership intervention. However, they form an unpredictable system and produce unreliable results. Comments such as "made progress" or "will continue efforts" lack rigor. They leave unanswered important questions such as "Just how much progress?" "What sort of efforts?" and "Are these efforts sufficient to meet critical deadlines?" Words alone are not enough to focus leadership intervention.

Monthly reviews are most powerful when they track the quantitative measures of success. These include the vital outcome measures as well as the strategy control measures. When leaders quantitatively track the whats and the hows, they can determine two things:

- *Are we implementing our strategies*? This can be determined by tracking the strategy control measures.
- *Are our strategies working*? This can be determined by tracking the outcome measures.

Factual answers to these two diagnostic questions convert every static business plan into a dynamic implementation *process* to accelerate change. They reinforce the principle that strategy implementation is an experimental process, one that can continually be improved through discovering what works, what fails, and why.

DIVIDE ANNUAL GOALS INTO MONTHLY PREDICTIONS

Many people understand the value of measurement. Yet month by month they review the same simple static end-of-cycle goal such as "reduce cost by 30 percent by the end of fiscal year" or "reduce billing errors by 50 percent by the fourth quarter." Despite frequent review, they lack a method to detect whether they are moving fast enough to meet their year-end goal. So they guess their way throughout the year.

To detect early warning signs, wise leaders divide their planned annual targets into twelve monthly incremental predictions. Month by month, they track their factual progress versus predicted speed.

The monthly prediction is rarely a straight linear projection to the annual target. The challenges unique to each gap will cause progress to vary throughout the year, sometimes with little or no visible improvement in the early part of the implementation cycle. Data collection, causal analysis, or critical approvals may retard or accelerate the change process. The more we candidly acknowledge the realities of the system complexity, the more accurate the predictions and fewer the surprises.

STANDARDIZE THE DEVIATION REPORTS

If failure information is so valuable, then why does such knowledge often escape prompt leadership attention? One answer is variation in reporting styles. *How* failure information gets communicated is a frequent cause of failed business objectives.

Take a look at your own business. How do you and others track, document, and report progress? Do you follow common procedures, or do reporting formats differ by person, function, level, or geographic region? Does everyone review with the same frequency? To what extent do reporting styles reflect the unique preferences of individual managers or the politics and power structure of the organization?

In many organizations, progress reports range from oral to written to elaborate audiovisual presentations. And the frequency of review varies from annual to quarterly to none at all. Content ranges from streams of unedited numerical computer printouts to pages of detailed technical project management charts to defensive jokes and dismissive waves of the hand by underperforming politically protected individuals.

Such variations in reporting protocols can choke the organization with its own failure information. Errors fail to teach and cannot be corrected when they are invisible, miscommunicated, not recognized, or not decipherable. Inconsistent reporting practices create barriers to individual, group, and organizational learning. They misdirect attention and precious resources. Rapid strategy deployment requires rapid access to strategic information in a common, easy-to-read format.

A BOWLING CHART VISUALLY TRACKS MONTHLY PROGRESS

To quickly focus leadership attention, some leaders adopt a simple standardized deviation report: *a bowling chart.* This two-page visual tool tracks monthly progress in quantitative terms. Named after the score card of the familiar recreational game, the bowling chart records the monthly misses, strikes, hits, and partial hits of interim efforts to achieve priority targets.

The bowling chart goes beyond a person's stated good intentions to display the *actual* changes in business performance and focus management attention on critical gaps. It standardizes, consolidates, and links deviations from plan to depict planned monthly increments, the factual rate of change, early deviations from expectation, the interrelatedness among deviations, and cumulative impact.

What does a bowling chart actually look like? Figure 4-1 illustrates one. It maps factual versus predicted performance against time in a monthly progress matrix. The months of the planning cycle run across the top of the chart. For each control measure, the responsible person documents the reference number, starting value, end-of-cycle target, monthly prediction, and sometimes a three-year or world-class target. The bowling chart tracks monthly and cumulative misses as it is possible to make plan one month yet lag on the cumulative (year-to-date) target because of prior misses.

On a rolling basis, the responsible person for each critical control measure updates the factual monthly and year-to-date performance. Then, with circles, color, or shading, he or she identifies any and all deviations from the monthly and year-to-date predictions. These monthly "flags" focus leadership attention throughout the planning cycle.

The most effective versions of the bowling chart contain only quantitative indicators, not deadlines or milestones. And a reference number visually links aligned efforts throughout the organization. The decimal in the reference number shows the hypothetical cause-and-effect relationships among key measures or indicators specified in the annual plan. For instance, indicators 1.1, 1.2, and 1.3 identify the vital few process measures intended to drive indicator 1.0. A date records the currency of the review.

The numbering system makes visible the linkage among the objectives, strategies, and measures to assess the full quantitative impact of individual deviations. It facilitates interim changes to the plan without having to redo the whole plan or wait until the next planning cycle. And it provides a visual reminder to focus on the few most important challenges.

The bowling chart separates fact from fiction. It goes beyond a manager's stated good intentions to display actual changes in system level performance. Valuable benefits include that it is:

- *simple*—it focuses attention for immediate leadership intervention;
- *flexible*—we can surgically modify the plan during the cycle without having to wait until the next planning cycle to change the whole plan;

FIGURE 4–1 A Sample Bowling Chart

Updated 9/27/01

Annual Objective No.	Performance Measure		TOTAL 1996	TOTAL 1997	**YTD 1998**	Jan	Feb	Mar
1.4	Inventory Turns	Plan Actual	 11.9	12.4 13.6	13.9 13.5	12.3 13.0	12.7 12.8	14.1 *11.8*
1.41	Raw Mat/WIP Inventory Turnover	Plan Actual	32.0 31.5	29.0 32.1	32.3 35.6	28.0 30.9	29.0 30.6	30.0 *27.2*
1.42	Finished Goods Turnover	Plan Actual	16.4 17.6	16.6 20.6	24.4 21.9	22.0 22.5	23.0 *22.0*	27.0 *20.7*
1.6	Shipping Forecast Accuracy (%)	Plan Actual			100 98	100	100 100	100 95
2.1	Cost of Quality	Plan Actual	 10.8	10.6 9.8	9.1 9.0	9.8 9.3	9.6 9.1	9.4 8.7
2.11	Internal Failure	Plan Actual		 3.3	3.1 2.7	3.3 2.6	3.2 2.1	3.2 2.1
2.2	Warranty Cost	Plan Actual		 2.1	1.9 *2.2*	2.1 *2.5*	2.1 *2.2*	2.0 *2.6*
3.1	First Time Fill Rate	Plan Actual	 97.0	97.2 98.4	98.5 98.5	98.5 99.0	98.5 98.8	98.5 *98.3*
3.2	Date Shipped Date Order Received	Plan Actual						
3.3	Date Consolidated Less Date Order Received	Plan Actual	**Monthly and Year-to-Date Deviations**					
4.1	Total Variance	Plan Actual						
4.11	Volume Variance	Plan Actual	**Complete a Corrective Action Form**					
4.12	Manufacturing Variance	Plan Actual						
4.20	Safety	Plan Actual						
	Gross Cost Per LB tracking	Actual						
	Gross Price Per LB tracking	Actual						

A Sample Bowling Chart (continued)

Apr	May	Jun	Jul	Aug	Sep	Oct	Nov	Dec	1998 Objective	World-Class Target
14.4 *13.3*	14.7 *13.8*	14.5 *14.0*	14.4 *14.1*	14.4 15.1	14.3	14.8	13.3	13.6	14.0	
33/0 35.5	35.0 36.4	35.0 40.6	34.0 40.0	34.0 43.3	29.0	32.0	26.0	27.0	33.0	
26.0 *21.3*	25.0 *22.3*	24.0 *21.4*	24.0 *21.7*	24.0 *23.3*	24.0	25.0	21.0	22.0	25.0	
100 100	100 *94*	100 100	100 100	100 100	100	100	100	100	100	
9.2 8.9	9.0 8.0	8.8 8.8	8.6 *10.1*	8.4 *9.2*	8.2	8.0	7.8	7.4	7.4	
3.1 2.6	3.0 1.8	3.0 2.4	2.9 2.9	2.8 2.0	2.8	2.7	2.6	2.5		
2.0 1.7	1.9 *2.2*	1.9 *2.0*	1.8 1.8	1.8 *2.6*	1.7	1.7	1.6	1.5	1.5	
98.5 99.5	98.5 *97.5*	98.5 98.9	98.5 98.9	98.5 *96.9*	98.5	98.5	98.5	98.5	98.5	
from Plan Are Marked in Red										
for Each Monthly Deviation										

- *speedy*—we can promptly diagnose the system impact of individual deviations, and the chart can be updated quickly;
- *auditable*—we can quickly assess collective progress for it displays under- and overachievements;
- *visible*—we can see the implications of change on other parts of the business.

These features keep the plan fresh and relevant in a changing environment.

BOX: Elicit Early Failure Information

- Track factual quantitative progress
- Divide annual objectives into monthly predictions
- Monitor strategy drivers as well as desired outcomes
- Focus on monthly deviations from prediction
- Standardize the deviation reports
- Evaluate measurable impact on other objectives

SUMMARY

The bowling chart provides a practical tool to detect early warning signs and focus leadership attention. It tells us how far and how fast we are moving and how far we are yet from our goals. But what do we do when we experience a monthly miss? If we already used our wisdom, experience, best judgment, and factual analysis to select our initial strategies and control measures, then how do we behave in the face of a factual deviation from expectation? This challenge leads us to the next chapter, where we learn how to study the predictions that did not come true to identify and install timely corrective action.

CHAPTER 5

WHY AM I OFF PLAN?

DIAGNOSE THE ROOT BARRIERS TO PROGRESS

The voyage of discovery is not in seeking new landscapes but in having new eyes.

—Marcel Proust

Monthly failures and deviations are like accident statistics. They report the number of accidents in the home, on the road, or at the workplace. However, they do not tell us *how* to reduce the frequency or severity of the problem. Deviations don't tell us where we went wrong, which assumptions were false, or which strategies need to be replaced with more effective ones. To change the numbers, we need to examine the false predictions, polices, norms, and assumptions that created the unhappy situation in the first place. Consider the following example.

I recently attended a monthly executive review at a small manufacturing company. Round-robin, each senior executive reviewed their department goals, reported their monthly deviations from plan, and described their corrective actions. When it came time for Joe, the vice president of finance, he stood before his peers and reported that he was behind on the monthly goal for accounts receivable, a key department goal identified during the annual planning process. His entire department had attended an annual convention for one full week and had dropped behind on their commitments. Confidently, Joe reported that his department was back on top of the situation and was working overtime to catch up. They would be back on plan next month.

Much to the surprise of the team, Mike, the vice president of operations, queried, "When did you discover that you were attending this conference?"

Joe acknowledged that his department had scheduled their attendance several months earlier.

"Then why did going to the conference interfere with your goals?" Mike queried.

"We didn't have back-up resources," Joe replied.

"And why was there no back-up?" Mike pursued.

Joe flushed, "We didn't think we needed one."

"Why didn't you think that?"

"Because we thought we could make it up with overtime, and we didn't."

"But isn't this a yearly conference, and aren't there other conferences scheduled for the remainder of this year?"

Joe shuffled his feet, looked embarrassed, and promised to examine his department's policies and procedures to identify a more permanent solution.

The group concluded several things that day: First, working overtime was a reactive quick fix aimed at the symptoms of a deeper problem and failed to install a fundamental solution. Second, the finance department needed a more rigorous analysis of department methods to identify a permanent solution and relieve the unhealthy overtime pressure on finance personnel. Finally, the finance department lacked full commitment to the monthly target as critical to the success of the organization. Attending a conference? Is that like "The dog ate my homework" excuse of schoolchildren? Such a superficial explanation was an attempt to avoid a more honest confession, a rigorous analysis of the problem, and a painful solution, things that the VP of finance had hoped to avoid. Joe wasn't the only executive who reported weak corrective actions in that meeting. Everyone learned that day just how far the executive team still had to go to take each monthly deviation seriously and conduct a thorough analysis to identify and install effective solutions.

APPLY CAUSAL ANALYSIS TO EVERY DEVIATION

Like the vice president of finance in this example, many people initially react to problems with short-term energy and actions. With a flurry of activity, they focus on *erasing the symptoms* of the problem rather than taking the time to identify and eliminate the fundamental structural issues that created the problem in the first place.

A fundamental solution always requires a factual causal analysis with attention to methods. Many people fail to conduct a thorough factual gap analysis. But, words alone ("We missed our target") and isolated numbers can obscure important trends and patterns hidden in the data. When people take the time to analyze the factual situation, they can better understand and address the exact nature of the problem.

Causal analysis is simply good management. In general terms, it says we will

- take responsibility for our errors,
- avoid a quick fix reaction,

- study the predictions that did not come true,
- manage with facts and data,
- identify the root barriers to progress, and
- make appropriate behavioral adjustments to prevent recurrence.

This process is sometimes called the *root cause problem-solving* process.

Over the last two decades, many companies spent large sums of money to train people in root cause problem-solving techniques. Unfortunately, these same companies failed to

- link root cause analysis to the achievement of *annual* objectives,
- enforce causal analysis *beyond* manufacturing personnel to demand the same rigor of other departments and the executive team,
- promote causal analysis as a professional *decision-making process*, not just a problem-solving process, and
- employ a *few* picture charts to communicate the final diagnosis.

These and other factors impede rapid strategy implementation.

Causal analysis is a critical *decision-making* skill that can improve every facet of business and personal life. It can systematically convert any performance gap into project direction, a midterm breakthrough into sequenced annual breakthroughs, an annual company goal into individual and departmental contributions, an individual goal into critical process improvements, and a monthly deviation into appropriate corrective action. Let's take a look at how wise leaders enforce causal analysis to minimize monthly deviations from prediction.

EXPOSE THE INDIVIDUAL'S LOGIC

Some people are reluctant to collect relevant data due to impatience or the mistaken belief that, because of their position or experience, they command all the answers.

Other people will provide data when asked. Yet, they avoid a causal analysis. We all know what it is like to attend a meeting or receive a memo where someone submits many columns or pages of data yet provides no analysis or conclusions. What are we supposed to understand? They leave the interpretation up to us. Perhaps they abdicate responsibility for causal analysis for fear of being wrong, delivering an unpleasant message, drawing an unpopular conclusion, or simply because they are lazy. The simple truth is that they have not studied the data and are wasting our time by shifting the burden to us to do it for them.

To shift the burden of thinking back to the source, wise leaders require individuals to exhaust their own problem-solving skills before asking for the help of others. They create a set of structures to ensure a fact-based causal analysis of any deviation from plan.

SIMPLIFY THE DECISION-MAKING PROCESS

Some people worry that the root cause decision-making process will be too complex or time-consuming. Graphical tools *can* feel awkward. Data *may* look unwieldy. And useful facts *may not* be easily accessible. For these and other reasons, wise leaders employ a *few* diagnostic questions and picture tools.

To simplify and accelerate the root cause decision-making process, some leaders adopt a standardized corrective action form. This simple one-page tool visually guides and summarizes the decision-making process and exposes the individual's logic in closing a measurable gap.

This is not a voluntary report. *Each month, every owner of a deviation must complete a corrective action form.* Three deviations in one month mean three corrective action forms. Many people think that they don't have to conduct a gap analysis unless they are off plan or experience a monthly deviation from prediction. But at the beginning of every planning cycle, *every* annual target or commitment describes a priority measurable gap that can benefit from causal analysis. The corrective action form informs and guides the decision maker on how to close any measurable gap.

SHOW DON'T TELL

A picture is worth a thousand words *and* numbers. So, to economize shared time, wise leaders refuse to react to tables of numbers, only pictures. They require that *everyone* employ a few standard graphical tools to convert numbers into the simple picture diagrams like the line graphs and bar charts that we see in daily newspapers and magazines. They organize and display the facts to illustrate the picture story, one that can be understood by a sixth-grade student. Figure 5-1 illustrates a pictorial version of the corrective action form.

Visual management and picture tools become especially important in a global management environment. When your manufacturing facility lies in Beijing, China, your distributor operates in Milan, Italy, and your marketing operation exists in Chicago, Illinois, fact-based pictures minimize language barriers and reduce the time it takes to decipher messages. They help to avoid misunderstanding, reduce

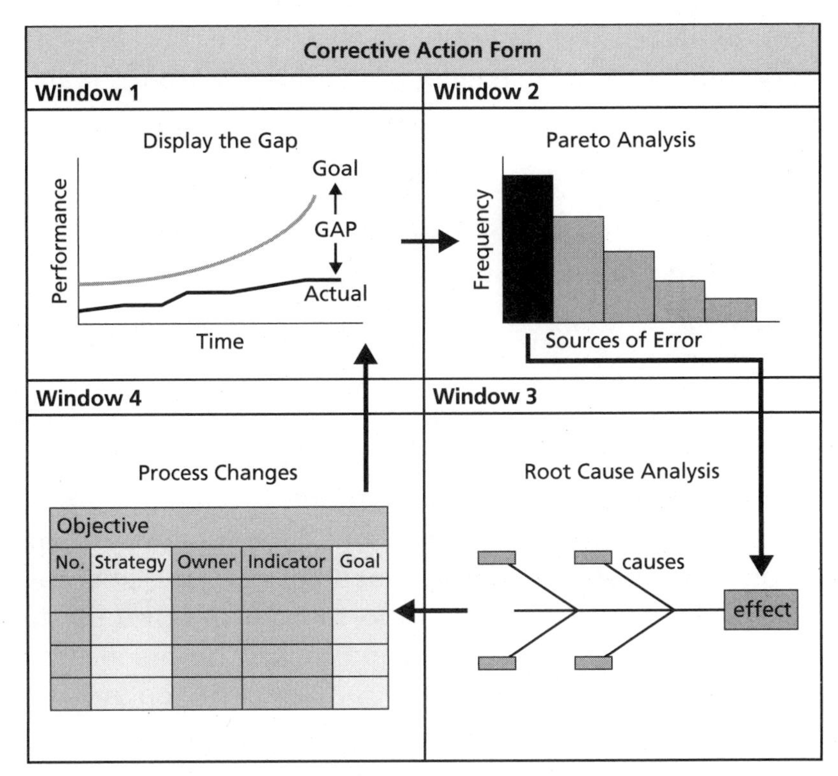

FIGURE 5-1 The Corrective Action Form Displays the Root Cause Analysis to Close the Gap

ambiguity, and align assumptions and strategies for running the business. When leaders speak with picture tools, they can communicate clear direction, explain the rationale behind strategic choices, and motivate coordinated action.

FOUR QUESTIONS GUIDE THE CAUSAL ANALYSIS

Unlike many versions of the root cause problem-solving template, the corrective action form provides a concise one-page visual summary of the gap analysis (see Figure 5-2 for a sample form). Note that four diagnostic questions guide appropriate action. And a single graphical tool displays the answer to each essential leadership question. The four "windows" reveal the individual's decision-making process:

- What is the quantitative gap?
- Where should I focus first?
- What is the root impediment to progress?
- What system changes will improve performance?

Some people question how much information they should display in each window. The answer is to share a few pictures to tell the story. From one month to the next, new knowledge will cause graphical charts to change. We may need to examine several charts before the story begins to emerge. Usually it takes only a few charts to summarize the discovery. Let's take a look at these visual diagnostic tools.

Window 1: What Is the Quantitative Gap? Collect the Dots and Plot the Dots

Events are often linked to a pattern of *behavior over time*. When we reflect on past experience, today's problem is often only the most recent event in a larger pattern of behavior. Various picture patterns include trends, a widening gap, oscillating behavior, random variation around a predictable level of performance, or a pattern with an anomaly.

The particular pattern often suggests a hidden structure at play. Predictable actions and reactions create system dynamics that produce predictable outcomes. Once we identify a pattern of behavior, we can take action to change the behavior pattern to meet our needs or expectations.

A *run chart* reveals the pattern of factual behavior over time (see window 1 in Figure 5-2). It displays variation, trends, or cyclical patterns. A control chart is a special kind of run chart with additional statistical calculations to define the range of expected variation under normal conditions and designate numerical warning limits for action. The action limit identifies any unusual event or deviation from expectation requiring leadership attention. Each chart places the interpretation of a single event into perspective from a structured system dynamic. To alter the pattern, we must look behind the dots to identify the hidden structured problems and limiting factors that control the outcomes.

Window 2: Where Should I Focus First? Test the Assumptions and Look for Differences

A pattern of behavior such as declining sales only shows us where we are suffering. It does not show us what we must change. To make fundamental change, we need to look behind the pattern to diagnose the dynamic structure creating the picture, a structure we can control.

One insightful technique is to sort or segment performance data by categories to focus leadership intervention on the source of our most frequent or severe troubles. The key word is *by*. Important insights emerge when we segment performance by size, frequency, cost, impact, geographic region, supplier, product or service type, and so forth. Categorical or subgroup differences in performance can show us where to focus first and shape our approach to the problem.

This kind of differentiation is sometimes called *Pareto analysis*. It is based on the Pareto principle

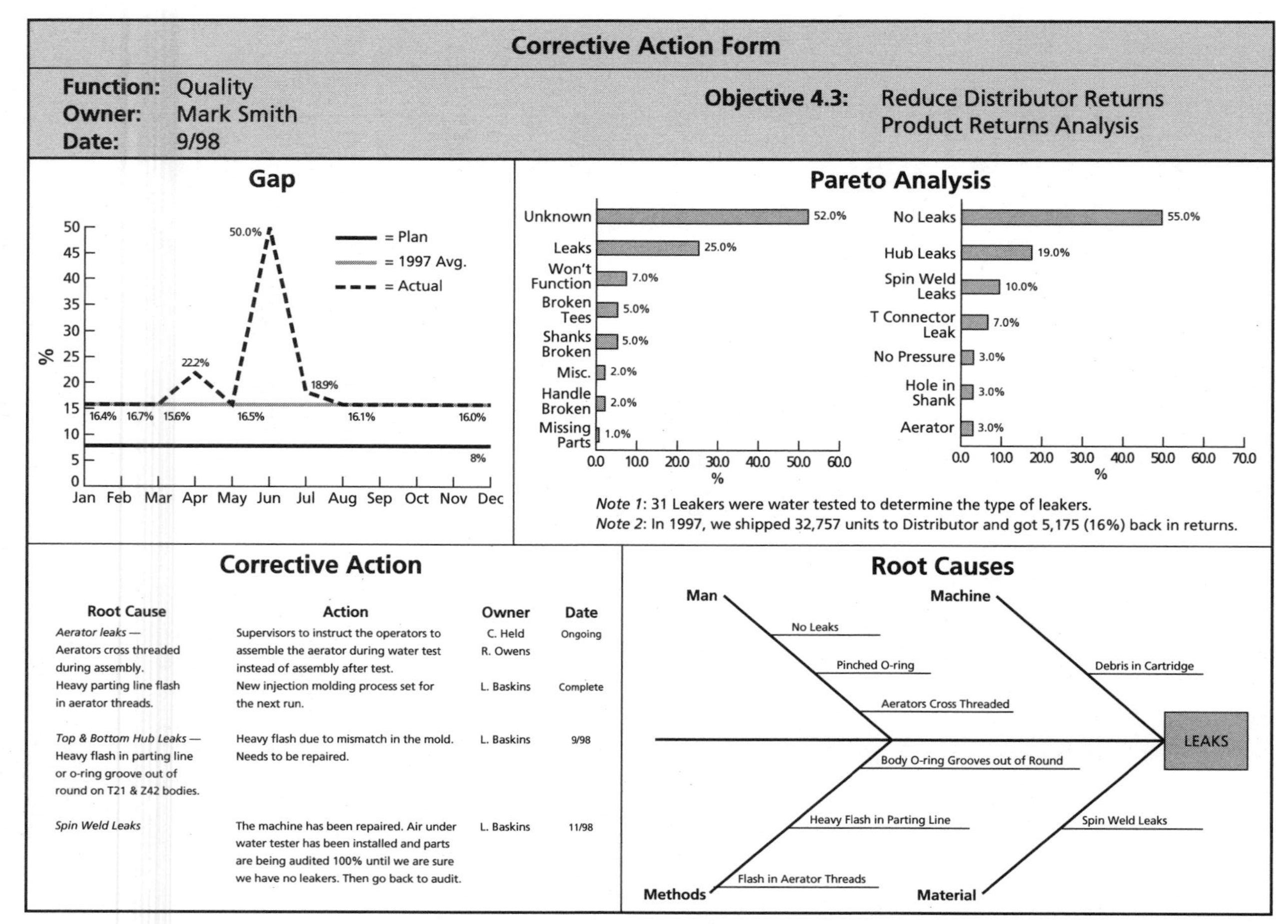

Corrective Action Form

Function: Quality
Owner: Mark Smith
Date: 9/98

Objective 4.3: Reduce Distributor Returns
Product Returns Analysis

Gap

Pareto Analysis

Note 1: 31 Leakers were water tested to determine the type of leakers.
Note 2: In 1997, we shipped 32,757 units to Distributor and got 5,175 (16%) back in returns.

Corrective Action

Root Cause	Action	Owner	Date
Aerator leaks — Aerators cross threaded during assembly.	Supervisors to instruct the operators to assemble the aerator during water test instead of assembly after test.	C. Held R. Owens	Ongoing
Heavy parting line flash in aerator threads.	New injection molding process set for the next run.	L. Baskins	Complete
Top & Bottom Hub Leaks — Heavy flash in parting line or o-ring groove out of round on T21 & Z42 bodies.	Heavy flash due to mismatch in the mold. Needs to be repaired.	L. Baskins	9/98
Spin Weld Leaks	The machine has been repaired. Air under water tester has been installed and parts are being audited 100% until we are sure we have no leakers. Then go back to audit.	L. Baskins	11/98

Root Causes

FIGURE 5-2 A Sample Corrective Action Form

that most of our problems derive from only a few of the reasons. The idea is that we should focus attention on the most frequent or highest impact issue as the most valuable opportunity. A Pareto chart is an ordered bar chart that displays the frequency, cost, or impact of a variable factor in order of highest to least (see window 2 in Figure 5-2). It displays, in decreasing order, the relative importance of each cause to the problem. By separating the critical few from the potentially less significant sources, we can identify corrective actions for maximum impact.

By stratifying or segmenting the data, we can test our most primitive assumptions about cause and effect. These basic "if" and "then" hypotheses influence our strategies. For example, if we are trying to increase the sales of life insurance, we might sort sales data to test the assumption: "If the customer is over age thirty, then we sell more life insurance than we do to those who are under thirty years of age." The number of life insurance policies organized and displayed by age group will either confirm or disprove this assumption enhancing the quality of subsequent actions.

A thorough gap analysis typically requires multiple layers of Pareto analysis. We can drill down and look for differences by product family, by product type, and then by the manufacturing facility of that product. Any similarities and differences will affect the focus and design of our strategies. And if the bars are the same height, then we continue to search for other distinctions and modify our strategies accordingly.

Window 3: What Is the Root Impediment to Progress? Diagnose the Hidden Limiting Factors

Once we choose where to focus leadership intervention (usually on the most frequent or severe sources of disappointment), we need to understand *why* we are experiencing problems in that narrow area of the business. This requires attention to the various structural elements that work to *maintain* the status quo.

Inhibiting factors are often invisible to the naive change agent because it often looks like nothing is happening, so resistance seems to come out of nowhere. This is especially true when there is a delay between cause and effect. For example, a layoff, rude management behavior, or a failure to respond to suggestions, even several years ago, can limit your ability to encourage others to take risks today.

To make and sustain significant progress, wise leaders take the time to identify and eliminate the hidden *root* impediments to change. This is not easy, because cause and effect are not often close in time or space. The initial visible problem is often only the symptom of a deeper, more complex cross-functional problem involving other departments and individuals. For example, a rigid personnel policy, contradictory performance incentives, poor hiring practices, or inadequate customer care may cause far-reaching problems across departments, business units, and geographical regions, including foreign subsidiaries. Even more challenging are the hidden implicit norms—for example, the real number of hours people work in contrast to the stated work week.

Whether it is stress level, workload, prices, costs, or supplier concerns, certain factors determine when "enough is enough" and will control our ability to change. When change is too much, they push back, or feed back, in the direction opposite of our desires.

One simple diagnostic method to identify the root barriers to progress is called the five whys. Next time you face a problem, ask "Why?" *five times*. As the manufacturing executive team experienced, the first question "Why do we have this problem?" usually elicits a "cover your tail" answer. The answer to the next "Why?" may just begin to expose the true nature of the problem. By the time you get to the fifth "Why?" you are usually down to the root cause(s) beyond your local territory or control. To create lasting change, you may need to confront soft issues like reward or recognition systems, communication processes, safety, hidden norms, or cultural expectations.

Another diagnostic technique is called the *fishbone diagram* because it looks like the skeletal remains of a fish (see window 3 of Figure 5-2). A fishbone diagram identifies and maps the hypothetical factors limiting progress. This tool can be used to display the multiple factors contributing to the development of the problem and suggest additional individuals to include in the decision-making process. The problem or the effect to be analyzed is written at the location of the fish's head. The hypothetical causes of the problem such as human resources, equipment failures, poor methods, inadequate materials or information are displayed as bones directly attached to the spine of the fish. Smaller bones record specific influences within each major cause. Subsequent data analysis confirms the *few* most important root causes.

Cause and effect are not always linear. Some factors influence one another in a circular relationship. To gain valuable insight and improve the quality and longevity of their change tactics, some people map these additional circular dynamics.

Window 4: What System Changes Will Close the Gap? Take Timely Corrective Action

The fourth and final window of the corrective action form records the solutions or actions we choose to close the factual gap displayed in window 1. This step in the problem-solving process discourages analysis paralysis. It forces the individual to make choices based on their new improved understanding of the business system.

The most effective corrective actions attack the root barriers to progress displayed in window 3 of the primary sources of error displayed in window 2. These solutions often install changes in routine methods and systems that keep the organization stuck at old levels of performance. A *process flow chart* is commonly used to display these new steps and methods for more favorable performance. We will learn more about these structural solutions in the next chapter.

The success of the solutions documented in window 4 can be verified by witnessing a change in factual behavior recorded in window 1. This brings us full circle in the scientific experimental process so necessary for reliable results. To close dramatic gaps, we plan our changes, implement the solutions, check to verify factual impact, and take action based on our newly found wisdom and experience.

SUMMARY

While many people initially wish to skip over the facts and rush straight to a "solution," in the end, slower *is* faster. Early causal analysis eliminates many false starts and inadequate strategies that prevent the organization from ever achieving its goals and objectives.

A simple corrective action form exposes the individual's problem-solving logic using pictures and numbers. It provides a useful mechanism to encourage everyone to study the priority gaps, understand the root cause dynamics that keep us trapped at old levels of performance, and point to the most promis-

BOX: Use Causal Analysis to Achieve Annual Objectives

- Focus on the disappointments
- Make visible the logic
  - Quantify and display the measurable gap
  - Use facts to verify the working assumptions
  - Identify the hidden root barriers to progress
  - Map new protocols and procedures to close the gap
- Keep it simple; show don't tell
  - A picture is worth a thousand words and numbers
  - Use a *few* graphs to summarize the story
- Become a professional
  - Standardize root-cause analysis as *the* decision-making process.
  - Apply causal analysis to all deviations from expectation
  - Enforce causal analysis at *all* levels of the hierarchy

ing areas for leadership intervention. But not all corrective actions are equal—which leads us to the next chapter. There we will learn how to select, install, and monitor the most effective countermeasures to increase the probability that we achieve our annual goals and deliver consistently superior results.

CHAPTER 6

WHAT CORRECTIVE ACTIONS HAVE I TAKEN?

MODIFY INADEQUATE METHODS

At all times it is better to have a method.

—Mark Caine

Frequent review can detect early failure information, and causal analysis can identify hidden barriers to progress. But sometimes, people get confused over just when to react and how to change the outcomes. Consider the following example.

John is a charismatic vice president of sales for a software design company. When the CEO raised his annual sales goal by 25 percent this year, John asked for and received additional budget to hire a large number of reps to help him "make the numbers." In his initial action plan, John assigned a regional sales quota to each rep, designed a healthy commission structure, sent all reps to several sales effectiveness training classes, and assigned them each to a mentor.

John believes in holding people accountable. He estimates that one out of three new reps will not perform at the level he needs; so he is closely monitoring individual performance. To this end, he is conducting high-pressure monthly reviews where he demands a detailed explanation for any and all deviations from monthly quota. He is focusing particular attention on orders in the pipeline as a leading indicator of sales.

Unfortunately, John is not getting the results that he needs. His meetings are intense and disheartening to his people. The reps are following the guidelines that John and their mentors provided them, but they are not getting the orders that John expects. One by one, in a long grueling meeting, John makes each rep explain why they missed their monthly sales quota using facts and data. He has already fired three reps.

To avoid embarrassment, many reps are now inventing orders. John doesn't understand why so many orders are not converting into sales. Each canceled order seems to have a different explanation, and performance is getting no better. But John is not giving up. For each canceled order, he is requiring some sort of corrective action.

FOCUS ON THE PROCESS, NOT THE GOAL

Many leaders such as John initially believe they must hold out a carrot like a sales goal to get people to perform. They believe that the *goal* motivates people to perform and that top-down pressure will accelerate progress and improve performance. So, they set monthly goals and then treat them like a critical action limit. Any deviation from target is treated with scrutiny, often with dire consequences for the personnel.

Such a review tactic rarely produces favorable results and reveals a poor understanding of the nature of variation and process control. John's monthly sales quota, an arbitrary percentage of prior sales, was set independent of the known natural capability of his recommended sales process. In the absence of a thorough understanding of the *natural variation* inherent in John's recommended sales protocols, holding his people accountable for any goal may only encourage them to become more efficient at doing the wrong things.

REFRAIN FROM TAMPERING IN RESPONSE TO VARIATION

Some variation is normal and does not require intervention at the event level. It comes from the random expected variation around a predictable average inherent in the existing system. For example, the human body temperature varies hourly around an average of 98.9. If we were to rush to the doctor with a temperature of 99.1, we could be *overreacting* to a normal expected variation only creating a wider swing in body condition.

This same "nontampering" rule is true for the office. Not every problem that walks into the office is a problem to be immediately solved at the individual or event level. Rather, the solution often requires attention to the underlying system within which the anecdote is happening.

Many leaders like John force people to explain variation that is actually normal for the design of the existing process. Had John examined the natural variability of sales history, he might discover that even though he is experiencing disappointing results, no single sales figure that his people are achieving is abnormal for the design of his recommended sales process. Rather, his process is performing normally and is ideally designed to deliver the observed outcomes. His people are making all the standard calls, making all the recommended visits, and achieving expected close ratios with no abnormality.

THE MOST EFFECTIVE CORRECTIVE ACTIONS REQUIRE A CHANGE IN BUSINESS METHODS

Focusing on individual performance or a seemingly unpleasant event can often make matters worse. This is especially true for the monthly progress review. If you force people to explain noise or a single deviation, they usually will. They will invent some meaningless explanation and most likely take action that will only make matters worse. Most likely, if I force *you* to stand before your peers, berate you, and demand that you explain why you didn't meet your quota, soon you will *never* miss a sales quota. You *will* go get orders! But they will be *false* orders that will cancel the next month.

This only further distorts the key performance measure and makes an inadequate process even worse. Focusing on the unhappy event only creates conditions that cause people to lie, and now, no one knows what is the normal variation. It becomes even more impossible to identify the appropriate action limit and detect critical changes in the process. All because no one wants to be embarrassed in a sales meeting.

"But we didn't meet our sales quota!" you might still cry. True, but most likely your *process* has not changed. Before you attack any individual person or sales figure, first verify that the process is *capable* of meeting the desired goal. You may need to change the lead generation process, the sales call process, or the marketing process to reliably deliver this new level of performance.

In short, *never* ask people why they are not meeting goal when you know that the process has not changed. Only when we install a new system can we expect to see a step shift in the effect of the new process design. Performance may not yet meet our goals, but the procedural changes will define a new "normal" that will surpass the old. We can then recalculate the action limit and assess the need for more process improvements.

Today, John and his people look beyond analyzing individual deviations from plan to routinely study and improve the *design* of the process and practices that keep them trapped at undesirable levels of performance. The dialogue and tone of their meetings are professional and positive. Important questions include "Are we still on schedule?" "Did the solution get implemented?" "Did the software get installed?" The emphasis is first on the *how*, then on the effect. Notice that John is no longer talking about the goal. He is discussing the new strategies, behaviors, protocols, and methods that change the agreed-on process.

DIAGNOSE THE NATURE OF THE VARIATION

As John learned, the exact outcome of any individual event is factually meaningless when we lack a clear understanding of the natural variation inherent in the process. Some variation is indeed abnormal and requires immediate attention at the event level. Other variation is predictably normal even if it is consistently inadequate to meet our needs.

To choose the most effective interventions, wise leaders first diagnose the *nature* of the variation:

- *Special cause variation* emerges from unusual or unpredictable *events* outside the limits of normal expectation such as human error, an unusual sequence of events, or a freak occurrence such as a computer breakdown or a truck accident. To produce *consistent* results, we must identify and remove the root cause of the unusual event, and then *standardize* new procedures. The appropriate action limit can be calculated from historical experience.
- *Common cause variation* derives from the *design* of the fundamental system including the routine methods and results that vary with statistical predictability. If only common causes are present, the process is said to be stable, consistent, and in control, even if inadequate. To change the overall *level* of performance, we must look beyond the individual person or event to *redesign* or change the process or routine activities.

To raise and sustain new levels of performance, we need to identify and minimize both kinds of variation (see Figure 6-1). One activity builds consistent outcomes by eliminating the root cause of any unusual event that disturbs normal variation. The other elevates the level of process capability by doing new things to achieve goals.

MAP THE PROCESS TO EXPOSE PROBLEMS AND IDENTIFY SOLUTIONS

Behind every performance gap, a set of routine procedures generate and maintain results. The design and flow of these activities determine the overall level of

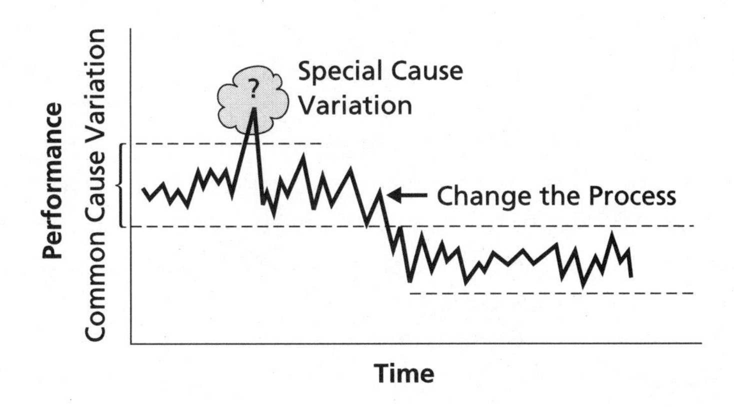

FIGURE 6-1 Understand Variation over Time before Taking Action

performance and customer satisfaction. Common limiting factors include

- inadequate knowledge of how a process *does* work;
- inadequate knowledge of how the process *should* work;
- variation in inputs and outputs (missing, late, or inadequate);
- poor flow (missing or unnecessary steps or bottlenecks);
- poor execution (human error, nonstandard procedures, unexpected events);
- delays due to reworking failures and idle "non-value-added" time; and
- excessive inventory, transportation, handling, or reporting.

Changing our behavior to eliminate such process problems improves quality, cost, speed, and delivery.

Process improvements install structural solutions that eliminate root impediments to progress. They derive from a factual causal analysis of the situation. And they change the business system. For example, if the diagnosis is inadequate information, then we may change the information subsystem or improve the data collection process. If unexpected changes in the environment adversely affect our business, then we may create a subsystem to anticipate changes, decrease sensitivity to change, or install countermeasures to prevent negative outcomes.

A process flow chart provides one simple picture tool to map a process or lack of a structured process within which anecdotes are occurring. This chart can be used to build consensus on procedural changes. Making visible the factual activity often strips the emotion out of a disturbing situation and provides an objective evaluation.

Teamwork improves the quality of the process map. The most accurate process maps reflect factual observation from many points of view. Three traditional process-mapping steps include document, standardize, and continuously improve, as detailed here:

1. *Document* the process to build consensus on the factual behavior.
   - Develop the "is" map to make visible the existing process.
   - Identify any undesirable variability.
   - Identify and analyze the "disconnects."
2. *Standardize* the "best" practices to create reliable desired results.

- Develop consensus on a "should" process.
- Specify the control measures.
- Monitor the control measures to detect unwanted variation.

3. *Continuously* improve the methods.
    - If the process is predictably inadequate to meet our improvement objectives, then *redesign* the process to elevate overall process *capability*.
    - Once again, standardize the new procedures to prevent backward slippage.

The aim is to increase reliability, effectiveness, and speed.

IDENTIFY NEW PROCESS CONTROL MEASURES

Process improvements often create the need for new control measures. These new indicators enable leaders to

- track adherence to agreed-on procedures (Are we doing what we said we would do?),
- assess the system level of performance (Are our changes working?), and
- provide evidence that the desired change has occurred (Did we close the factual gap?)

This new instrumentation brings us full circle to the very gaps that we aim to close. It defines a new set of control measures to monitor and control "how" we will achieve and sustain the critical system levels of performance specified in our annual objectives.

VERIFY CAUSE AND EFFECT

The most effective corrective actions derive from a factual gap analysis and will attack the root cause barriers to change. They will install structural changes. They will generally *not* be actions that create, react to, or gamble on singular events or individual persons. Rather, they will describe new protocols and procedures that can be monitored for consistent desirable results.

A quick review of the third and fourth windows of the corrective action form will suggest the quality and effectiveness of our new improved system. In one glance, we can verify whether the selected corrective actions

- attack the root limiting factors (Does every root cause identified in window 3 have at least one or more structural or procedural changes aimed at it?)
- install a structural change (Do these corrective actions standardize or redesign a routine process?)
- reduce variation (Do these corrective actions create consistent outcomes?)
- eliminate delays (Do these corrective actions increase speed?)
- focus attention (Are the corrective actions few in number?)
- provide sufficient impact (Will these corrective actions close the factual gap displayed in window 1?)

These criteria increase the likelihood that we will apply our precious time, energy, and resources on the most valuable improvement opportunities. The resulting corrective actions will modify the initial action plan based on the lessons learned.

BOX: How to Get Out of a Vicious Circle

Be truthful in answering these questions!

- Is there a structural process at work here? If so, which one?
- Am I shifting the burden? What is the underlying fundamental action that I am not willing to make or do not perceive myself to be able to do? Why?
- What is the symptomatic reactive quick fix I am about to take? What are the long-term consequences of these actions?
- What is my time horizon? Two, three, or six months down the road, will I be doing more of the same? What is the behavior over time?
- If I really tell myself the truth, what is the long-term cost? What is it I really want to do and am willing to do?
- Am I pushing people or removing the limiting factors?
- Where can I eliminate delays?
- Am I creating, reacting to, or gambling on events?
- Have I analyzed the situation from event, behavior-over-time, and structural points of view?
- What unintended side effects may emerge due to my changes?

SUMMARY

The study of special cause and common cause variation in performance increases the power of review. It eliminates false starts, improves the quality of action, and accelerates the change process. It suggests specific procedural changes that will elevate and sustain new levels of performance.

Despite the benefits of causal analysis, some people still refuse to conduct routine evaluations. They do not want to take the time to study deviations from plan, identify, or install structural solutions. They simply can't resist the tendency to skip over the causal analysis and rush straight to a quick fix.

Many failed objectives occur because the leadership never takes the time to verify that everyone is correctly practicing the recommended review procedures. They falsely assume that people are controlling their calendar, routinely analyzing failure information, and making appropriate process improvements. However, naively assuming that individuals will do what they are asked to do, trained to do, or convinced to do can be costly when the stakes are high.

How can you ensure that everyone is following the recommended review practices, including frequent review and early causal analysis of performance gaps? How can you verify that people are developing and installing reliable structural solutions? How can you continually improve collective review practices over time? These questions lead to the final part of this book, where you will learn how to ensure the consistent practice of these best review principles.

PART III

CONDUCT EFFECTIVE REVIEWS

IN PARTS I AND II, we learned the fundamentals of effective review. We can accelerate any change process when we identify the vital few measures of success, routinely track deviations from plan, study the predictions that did not come true, and take timely appropriate corrective action. But common sense does not make common practice. Sometimes people work in an environment where

- a boss does not enforce or reward disciplined review practices;
- there is no mechanism to verify adherence to recommended procedures; or
- best practices are not shared, evaluated, or continuously improved.

These and other factors limit everyone from reaping the enormous benefits of widespread continual review of annual goals and objectives.

How can you ensure that everyone conducts frequent reviews and responds to early warning signs with timely appropriate corrective action? One answer is *mandatory peer review*. In many organizations, performance reviews take place between boss and subordinate, often behind closed doors. This limits individual, group, and organizational learning: Adherence to agreed-on review procedures cannot be verified. Critical information fails to flow across the organization. Faulty assumptions go unchallenged. Valuable resources remain undiscovered. Incompatible strategies go unnoticed and are never reconciled. And collective progress cannot be quantified. In contrast, frequent peer review develops group intelligence and accelerates strategic action.

Peer review accelerates progress for many reasons:

- peer pressure is far more effective than top-down pressure for change,
- anticipation of public exposure minimizes delays and unnecessary failure due to inaction,
- many sets of eyes keep individual activities aligned with priorities,
- early consensus on "best" practices optimizes resources,
- different viewpoints improve the quality of information and the power of solutions, and
- previously unknown resources become known.

The promise of peer review goes beyond the informal boss–subordinate review behind closed doors. It may be easy to bluff the boss or another individual; however, it is difficult to bluff six or seven other intelligent coworkers whose objectives depend on you delivering yours. Also, while you may get away with excuses one month, the team gets smarter every month. Month in and month out, they become less likely to tolerate inadequate individual preparation.

On the positive side, people want to be liked and admired for a job well done. This motivates people to work hard and well for themselves and to assist others. When a team commits to shared goals and objectives, everyone looks forward to sharing and learning about issues affecting overall progress. It also becomes easier to maintain commitment despite adversity.

Part III describes three techniques for peer review that stimulate appropriate change:

- Standardize the prework to accelerate action and *individual learning*, the process by which individuals privately test assumptions, acquire new concepts, and modify personal behaviors prior to review.
- Control the dialogue to accelerate *group learning*, the process by which members share knowledge, test assumptions, develop consensus on preferred methods, and influence others to improve the quality of choice.
- Conduct an annual review to accelerate *organizational learning*, the process by which individuals and groups consciously alter explicit and implicit cultural norms to improve the reliability of the entire planning and implementation process.

The first technique reduces delays among ideas, individual action, and knowledge of the consequences. The second reduces delays in knowledge exchange. The third reduces delays in aligning people with the plan and the plan with critical changes in the environment. Such a learning enterprise, perhaps more accurately called an "unlearning" enterprise, openly and routinely confronts and replaces false assumptions and undesirable behaviors and norms with more effective ones in the spirit of continuous improvement.

CHAPTER 7

HOW DO I PREPARE FOR THE MONTHLY REVIEW?

STANDARDIZE INDIVIDUAL PREPARATION

Myth associates leadership with superior position. It assumes that when you are on top you are automatically a leader. But leadership is not a place, it is a process.

—James M. Kouzes and Barry Z. Posner

How many times do you attend meetings where people arrive late, lack a critical piece of information, possess too few copies for team review, or repeat boring defensive stories with no facts to back them up? If you are like many people, the answer is often. Consider the following example.

I recently observed a monthly department meeting at a small health services center in New England. The company was preparing to merge with another facility, and everyone was preparing, psychologically and financially, for a more professional organization. The head of operations, Derrick, had a respectful relationship with his five direct reports. Everyone had measurable objectives. And everyone had been trained in leadership, root cause problem-solving techniques, and time management.

The meeting was scheduled for 10 A.M., and although it was now eight minutes past the hour, members of the team were still arriving with coffee, muffins, and papers. As they selected chairs and settled into their places, Derrick, an affable fellow, passed out an agenda showing who would go first and what topics would be discussed in the next hour. For several of the attendees, this was their first look at the schedule for the morning.

Derrick's meeting began with unfinished business from the last meeting, followed by three topics requiring a team decision: the termination of a lower-level employee, the schedule for the upcoming annual company picnic, and the purchase of some company vehicles. After several minutes of animated conversation, the group postponed two of the three topics to the next meeting due to inadequate information. Following a brief pause, the meeting continued with each team member reporting budget versus plan.

Mary-Ann, the manager of customer service, spoke quickly about sending her new hires to a training class and then left the meeting to get copies of an analysis of customer complaints requested by Derrick. Paul, the purchasing manager, in a barely audible voice, struggled to explain what he was doing to minimize late deliveries from an important vendor. And JayJay, a witty guy in transportation services, joked and laughed his way through his staff troubles. The two remaining members periodically darted in and out of the meeting to obtain supporting documents from their subordinates. With only ten minutes left, the team pulled out their annual objectives and casually discussed the need for more rigorous analysis. As the clock struck 11, three of the members left their chairs to attend other meetings, and two members stayed behind to review some detailed analyses. Derrick dutifully made a note of all unfinished business to begin the next monthly department meeting. Then the meeting officially ended.

DEFINE AND ENFORCE PREPARATION

Effective meetings require individual preparation. This means arriving on time, every time, with the essential information in an easy-to-share format. The more thorough the preparation, the more speedy and productive the review.

Some leaders, like Derrick, expect everyone to know what to provide and how to present information. They publish agendas, advocate teamwork, train people in problem-solving skills and time management, and preach the need for local leadership. Then they indulge poor preparation, permit numerous distractions, and allow, if not invite, miscellaneous "housekeeping" details to dominate precious shared time. Such practices impede the implementation of any plan.

Wise leaders leave little to chance. They understand that group intelligence depends on the contributing intelligence of individuals. So they define and enforce premeeting protocols to improve the quality of shared time. They go beyond *telling* people how to prepare for review meetings to install a reliable structured premeeting *process* to accelerate individual learning and right action.

Shared time is a precious resource best spent on the things people can't figure out for themselves. To the extent that individuals exhaust their own problem-solving skills before the meeting, the more full the benefits of joint inquiry. Figure 7-1 provides a generic template for standard prework requirements.

FIGURE 7-1 Standardize the Prework Requirements

PRIOR TO THE REVIEW

Diagnose and correct deviations from expectation.

1. Know where you are off plan
   - Publicly display each measure using a run chart or control chart.
   - Identify positive and negative deviations from plan (performance, resources utilized, and schedule).
2. Know where the problem occurs.
   - For each deviation, segment the data (by location, by size, by age, etc.).
   - Conduct multiple levels of Pareto analysis.
   - Select the focus for investigation.
3. Know why you are off plan.
   - Use a group process to brainstorm multiple causes of the focused problem.
   - Identify and document the vital few (no more than three) root cause(s) of the focused problem.
   - Use statistical tools to validate the root causes.
4. Take timely corrective action.
   - For each root cause, implement immediate and permanent fixes.
   - Verify that fixes satisfy initial resource and time parameters.
   - Assign owners and deadlines.
   - Tie corrective actions to a revised action plan.
5. Document new knowledge.
   - Update quantitative progress on the bowling chart.
   - Circle all deviations, monthly and year-to-date.

- For each and every deviation, document the gap analysis on a corrective action form.
- Assess the quantitative impact of corrective actions.
- Make copies of bowling charts and corrective action forms for each team member.

6. Set priorities for the group review.
   - Identify the deviations of highest concern to you and others.
   - Quantify future implications.

EXHAUST INDIVIDUAL PROBLEM-SOLVING SKILLS PRIOR TO THE GROUP MEETING

Three thinking *questions* guide individual preparation. Developed in Part II of this book, these diagnostic questions model a professional problem-solving process:

- Where am I off plan?
- Why am I off plan?
- What corrective actions have I already taken to close the gap?

The answers to these questions are not anecdotal. Rather, individuals conduct a factual causal analysis to support their conclusions and justify the rationale for their actions. An updated bowling chart visually reports factual deviations from prediction. And a completed corrective action form for each deviation displays the rigor of the logic for the specific corrective actions already taken. These two standard reports define the *deliverables* or prerequisites for monthly group attendance.

The bowling chart and corrective action form force individuals to use their intelligence, reach conclusions, and make choices *prior to* the meeting. Too often people bring all of their working documents to group meetings. They do not distill their information and leave it up to the group to interpret the information and draw their own conclusions. This is an abuse of other people's time and an evasive way of avoiding responsibility for individual action. A standard reporting format clarifies expectations in advance and shifts the peer review from one of a "data dump" to a professional justification of conclusions and rationale for current strategies. The group can then evaluate the perceived effectiveness of the individual's corrective actions.

DISPLAY THE CAUSAL ANALYSIS

Enforcing prior causal analysis is very different from the way many people conduct reviews. Often, people come to a meeting prepared to learn of results and brainstorm ideas. The essential dialogue is "Where are we? Oh, no! What are we going to do now?" In contrast, premeeting diagnosis of failures accelerates appropriate individual action and improves the quality of shared time. Requiring that each participant complete the prepared questions shifts the burden of obtaining important tactical knowledge back to the responsible individuals. The atmosphere in the meeting shifts from passively bemoaning lagging information about disappointing outcomes to *acting* on leading information about the effectiveness of *strategies.* The review dialogue shifts to "This is what we have learned, and this is what we are doing about it. How can we be even more effective?" Participants then share facts and resources to minimize further errors and delays.

Some people wait to experience a monthly miss before they conduct a causal analysis. But, such a *reactive* approach to solving problems again wastes precious time and valuable information. At the beginning of the year, *every* annual goal defines a gap that requires a proactive causal analysis to test and modify the false assumptions and behaviors that prevent us from performing at a level consistent with our vision. The more thorough the gap analysis, the more effective our tactics and strategies.

In the early months following the adoption of premeeting deliverables, it is not uncommon to see people scurrying around gathering data, drawing hasty charts, and making last-minute communications. Over time, however, individuals establish natural premeeting activities that systematically advance causal analysis. What begins as a primarily reactive problem-solving response to monthly deviations evolves into a more proactive decision-making process where causal analysis becomes a way of life. "Management by fact" replaces "management by miracle," and the display of charts and graphs in offices, hallways, and the shopfloor provides additional impetus for change. When people routinely manage with facts and picture tools, the monthly review becomes a "come as you are" meeting where factual progress is updated on standard reports and supporting charts come off the wall.

REPORT CORRECTIVE ACTIONS *ALREADY* TAKEN

Many people collect data, study their failures, and identify the root barriers to progress. Then, however, they stall out debating the merits of alternative scenarios for success. Many of these same people come to review meetings with promises or ideas of what they *intend* to do to solve the problem.

Ideas, alone, can masquerade as a tactic to procrastinate and delay the pace of change. Too often people use the excuse of waiting for someone else's approval when they could have taken earlier appropriate action and did not. Such "planned helplessness" only creates unnecessary delays in progress.

To get the show on the road, wise leaders *force individual choice*. They understand that people choose to change themselves, so they deliberately create conditions under which natural and appropriate change can take place. They use their premeeting procedures to encourage people to convert the partially known into the definable and to stimulate right action.

One simple technique is to require individuals to bring to the peer review a list of corrective actions they have *already taken* to get back on plan. The key words are already taken. This simple deliverable backed by causal analysis stimulates individuals to take right action and exhaust their creative energy prior to the meeting. Group members can then evaluate whether the individual's changes are sufficient to close the gap and sustain progress.

"But doesn't this put people on the spot?" you might ask. It certainly does! And that is precisely why this premeeting requirement accelerates strategy deployment. The simple but effective premeeting question ("What corrective actions have you already taken?") kicks people from the check phase to the act phase of the plan-do-check-act cycle for continuous improvement. It activates an experimental learning process to improve the quality of strategies and minimize delays between theory, action, and knowledge of the consequences. When we take action, we redefine "before" and "after." Through personal choice we change the boundaries of experience. We gain valuable insight and discover previously unknown capabilities as we restructure skills and resources along the way.

Many people worry that they cannot collect or analyze sufficient data within a one-month period to report appropriate or sufficient corrective action. Yet this reflects too narrow an interpretation of corrective action. Sometimes factual research and causal analysis do require an extended analysis period. The important thing is to share interim conclusions on a rolling basis. From month to month, corrective actions will reflect new knowledge gained from the continual analysis of failure information.

REWARD AND RECOGNIZE ADHERENCE TO "BEST PRACTICES"

Many people wonder how the monthly review of annual goals will affect their individual evaluation at the end of the year. However, recall that the monthly review is not a review of personnel. Rather, it tracks strategic progress throughout the planning cycle.

Rapid strategy deployment needs the support of the human resources function in such vital areas as evaluation, development, and training. A close examination of the performance appraisal system may reveal that it is poorly linked with the business priorities. Often it has its own agenda. The more closely it aligns with the strategy implementation, the more rapid and dramatic the change.

To minimize the number of failed goals and objectives, wise leaders align their personnel appraisal system with the strategy deployment system. This does not mean that individuals are penalized for missed targets, for every individual will experience missed targets. Rather, these leaders evaluate individual adherence to the *recommended* planning and review practices. They assess whether people are improving their skills in communication, causal analysis, and process improvement—all behaviors by which the organization hopes to achieve its desired objectives. By adhering to recommended *behaviors*, deviations will be minimal and educational in nature.

Again the emphasis is on the implementation *process*, not just the results. Key behaviors to recognize, reward, and discipline at the individual level include the following:

- Adherence to the monthly review schedule ("Have you conducted twelve monthly reviews with your peers and subordinates?")
- Adherence to premeeting protocols ("Were your action plans, bowling charts, and corrective action forms complete?")
- Quality of the causal analysis ("Are you skillfully using graphical tools like the run chart, Pareto chart, and process flow chart?")
- Continuous improvement ("What are your personal weaknesses in planning, implementation, and review skills, and what are you doing about it?")

The more clear the expectations during the monthly review, the more likely that best practices will create reliable results.

LINK TRAINING RESOURCES WITH THE STRATEGY DEPLOYMENT PROCESS

When people are held accountable for measurable commitments and routinely subjected to peer review, they frequently demand more training with more rigorous content. Unfortunately, in many organizations, training topics are general and fail to explicitly support the planning and deployment process or the strategic objectives.

Rapid strategy implementation requires that members gain easy access to any and all skills training needed to complete the key steps in the planning and review cycle. Supporting topics include causal analysis, process improvement, time management, and listening skills. People also need training in how to use the tools of strategy deployment such as action plans, bowling charts, corrective action forms, and other company-specific protocols for setting priorities and aligning activities and resources with the high-level objectives.

To align existing training resources with the critical skills needed for successful implementation, some organizations create a training matrix. Key planning, deployment, and review steps are outlined on one axis, the existing training resources on the other. A second matrix can compare training resources with specific technical skills needed for the specific breakthroughs. A quick visual review directs people to valuable existing resources such as root cause problem-solving training or courses in process control. Any holes or empty cells highlight opportunities for additional training.

Over time, the training material often becomes more applied than theoretical and more real-time than "case study" as people often arrive at class with their bowling charts and corrective action forms in hand.

BOX: Define and Enforce Individual Preparation

- Exhaust individual problem-solving skills before the meeting
  - Apply causal analysis to annual objectives
  - Record and display the causal analysis
  - Document the corrective actions *already* taken
- Reward and recognize adherence to "best practices"
- Link training resources to the strategy implementation process

SUMMARY

The promise of peer review stimulates individuals to make timely appropriate change. When people know they will be held accountable and evaluated by others, they often take their responsibilities more seriously and activate changes to demonstrate measurable achievements. And clear expectations for preparation improves the quality of shared time.

While the benefits of peer review are undeniable, some people worry that group meetings will invite blame or run out of control. In the next chapter, we will learn how to control the group dialogue to create a safe yet candid public forum to confront weak assumptions, modify inadequate strategies, and leverage previously hidden resources, all in the spirit of continuous learning.

CHAPTER 8

HOW DO WE CONDUCT THE MONTHLY REVIEW?

CHALLENGE THE FACTS AND ASSUMPTIONS

Facts often kill a good argument.

—Brian L. Joiner

Many people believe that an effective team review is primarily a reporting process where individuals communicate factual progress and confirm that they are taking timely appropriate corrective action. But, a progress report alone is merely knowledge *transfer*, which implies a one-way communication. It ignores the valuable knowledge that can be gained through interactive dialogue and shared insight.

Individual learning is *not* the same thing as organizational learning. What individuals learn often remains a hidden resource for the organization. People often "know" but do not effectively channel their knowledge to others who can benefit. Consider the following obstacles in your own organization:

- Have you ever concealed knowledge of conflicts or problems from your supervisor or peers because they were "undiscussable"?

- Have you withheld negative information from someone during a meeting for fear of a confrontation or retaliation?
- Have you ever relied on the ambiguity of existing policies to avoid dealing directly with someone or something?
- Have you ever withheld fears about the effectiveness of someone else's strategy or competence?

Interactions like these create and reinforce conditions for error. While individuals may know or have learned, the organization does not. Otherwise creative bright individuals become incapable of correctly diagnosing and replacing inadequate practices and strategies with more effective ones.

To optimize the power of peer review, wise leaders take controlled steps to facilitate knowledge *exchange*, the process by which one party exchanges knowledge of a problem with others for help in the design of a "best" solution. They follow a few standard procedures to rapidly uncover, challenge, and modify deeply rooted assumptions and dysfunctional behaviors that keep people stuck at undesirable levels of performance. Multiple minds can clarify vague misunderstandings, reveal new information, identify previously unknown resources, and improve the quality and aggressiveness of corrective actions. Supportive conditions promote rapid *shared* learning.

USE STANDARD PROTOCOLS TO FACILITATE KNOWLEDGE EXCHANGE

Some people worry that a group review will take too long or become dysfunctional. This can be true. Domineering individuals, heated disagreements, unfavorable news, and boring monologues can cause a group meeting to spin out of control. These and other distractions frequently occur when a leader conducts an unstructured meeting with inadequate ground rules.

The most effective group reviews follow a set of structured protocols and procedures. These standard practices define and control such key variables as

- reporting format,
- decision rules, and
- attendance.

A disciplined peer review creates shorter more energetic meetings, more aggressive corrective actions, and more rigorous factual analysis for an accelerated coordinated pace of change. Let's take a look at some of these disciplined behaviors.

FOCUS *ONLY* ON DEVIATIONS FROM PLAN

Group time is a precious resource for solving the most pressing problems of the business. Unfortunately, many reviews waste valuable time on presentations emphasizing where managers are *on plan.* Problems, when detected, remain poorly investigated. And willful ignorance sets in.

When we ignore problems, we avoid solutions. For this reason, the most effective reviews focus attention on those things that people cannot solve on their own. These problem areas typically emerge as factual deviations from plan. Deviations from expectation can include

- actual versus predicted performance,
- magnitude of resources utilized versus allocated resources, and

- factual schedule relative to the planned time frame.

The more quickly we can elicit failure information, the more easily we can diagnose and eliminate root barriers to progress.

To focus leadership intervention, wise leaders encourage the public analysis of failure during peer reviews. This is not an informal discussion of problems. Rather, the leaders dispense with presentations of where people are on plan to focus *only* on where people are *off plan.* They replace passive presentations, where people spend most of their time listening, with an active problem-solving session focused on closing critical gaps (e.g., the monthly deviations from expectation).

Each month, deviations may emerge in the priority measures for daily management or annual breakthrough targets. To maintain an agressive schedule, many leaders allocate shared time in favor of the breakthrough challenges. They quickly review their financial results and their business fundamentals since these measures reflect the historical organization. Then they devote the greater part of their time to their future-oriented breakthrough challenges. The allocation of time may look like this:

- 20 to 30 percent historical focus (review business fundamentals and financial results), and
- 70 to 80 percent future focus (review breakthrough strategies)

By emphasizing the stretch priorities, the leadership reinforces the concept that we must continually apply creativity and innovative thinking to bridge the vision gap.

CHALLENGE THE RIGOR OF THE CAUSAL ANALYSIS

Many people fret when they first learn that the group monthly review will focus *only* on deviations. They believe that making visible the failures will depress and discourage people. This is understandable. For when results are off the mark, many people blame others. But blame is never part of the solution. We achieve far better results when we analyze and improve the *process*—the methods, protocols, or procedures that got us into trouble in the first place. When we conduct a calm factual causal analysis of the routine methods, the *how* rather than the who, we can create a safe honest environment to solve problems in a sustainable way.

To get beyond the blame, effective reviews emphasize the quality of causal analysis as being critical to achieving every objective. Peers work together to improve the logic by which individuals make decisions and choose tactical strategies. They encourage one another to improve self-evaluation skills and to analyze failure and determine the cause of a mistake.

The monthly review provides a most valuable coaching opportunity to develop causal analysis in the context of annual objectives. Each month, peers review the individual's predictions that did not come true and the corrective actions they have already taken to ascertain the true lessons and guide the individual for maximum learning. Through this coaching process, peers teach others how to be professionals and remind each other that effective leadership for rapid strategy deployment depends on knowing the capabilities of people and systems to minimize problems and accurately predict outcomes.

FIGURE 8-1 Standardize the Review Meeting Protocols

DURING THE REVIEW

Verify that corrective actions are necessary and sufficient to get back on plan and sustain progress

1. Convene as a team.
   - Establish a review schedule.
   - Adhere to the review schedule.
2. Distribute prepared progress reports.
   - Distribute updated bowling charts.
   - For each deviation, distribute a corrective action form.
3. Proceed in round-robin fashion. Silently review the corrective action reports.
   - As a group, silently review the individual's bowling chart.
   - Silently, note any and all quantitative deviations from plan.
   - Starting with the first deviation, conduct a three-minute silent review of the gap analysis and corrective actions. Avoid wasting valuable time presenting where you are on plan.
4. Ask data-driven questions.
   - Collectively and sequentially review the four windows of the individual's corrective action form.
   - Finalize group observations and questions on each window of the corrective action form before moving to the next window.
   - Identify opportunities to improve the causal analysis.
   - Ask the individual to clarify, add, or modify corrective actions.

5. Report upward any significant deviations from plan ("back on plan next quarter," "off annual target").
   - Anticipate future obstacles.
   - Predict quantitative impact of the corrective actions.

VERIFY QUANTITATIVE IMPACT

So, what exactly does a group monthly review look like? Deviations form the starting point. In round-robin style, each person reports any and all deviations backed up by a factual gap analysis prepared according to premeeting standards. To avoid distractions, anecdotal stories, and subjective opinions, participants control the meeting dialogue to focus on the rigor of the gap analysis and corrective actions. Specifically, peers review the individual's answers to the three diagnostic questions ("Where am I off plan?" "Why am I off plan?" "What corrective actions have I already taken?") developed in Part II of this book. Then they critique the logic behind the answers. (Figure 8-1 provides a generic template for conducting a peer review.)

The team collectively owns the answer to the question "Do we believe that this individual's corrective actions are necessary and sufficient to close the gap and sustain performance?" This high-level question highlights four key issues:

- *Necessary*? Do the countermeasures factually attack the root cause? Are they few in number?
- *Sufficient*? What is the quantitative impact of the corrective actions taken? Are these actions aggressive enough to close the gap? Are contingency plans in place?

- *Sustainable*? Do the countermeasures install reliable repeatable process improvements or one-time quick-fix events?
- *Aligned*? How do the process changes affect others in the organization?

The answers to these questions begin an active dialogue and creative collaboration to accelerate the pace of change.

ABOLISH PRESENTATIONS

Many people become so enamored with their new skill at graphical display that they wish to share every detail of their causal analysis with their peers. I have attended many meetings where people described every minor bone of every moderate-sized bone of every large bone on their fishbone diagram and read to us every bar from every ordered bar chart in their Pareto analysis. We could see and believe that the individual had indeed engaged in a thorough gap analysis, but we really didn't need to see or hear the details of the working documents. We spent more time *listening* to the presentation than *thinking* about the problem. Directed or distracted by the presenting individual, we lacked the opportunity to think for ourselves and aid individual and group learning.

For this reason, the monthly group review is *not* a presentation! Rather, *it is a question-and-answer session* focused on solving elusive problems, not avoiding them. Specifically, group members ask questions to challenge the rigor of the factual analysis and stated corrective actions. In short, the individual is a respondent, not a presenter!

ENFORCE A BRIEF AND CONTROLLED SILENCE

How can peers limit the tendency to pontificate? One answer is the controlled use of silence. Silence can focus leadership attention and speed the thinking process to dramatically reduce meeting time.

To speed the thinking process, some leaders consciously apply silence as part of the group meeting structure. For each deviation, the individual leads a group silence of three minutes during which peers review the quality of the corrective action analysis. Following a shared silence, the individual still does not speak. Rather, team members ask questions, step by step, as they move clockwise through each of the four windows of the corrective action form, starting with window 1. They ask a set of standard diagnostic questions to quickly evaluate the

- size of the remaining gap,
- rigor of the factual analysis,
- credibility of the root barriers, and
- power of corrective actions already taken.

Figure 8-2 lists some simple diagnostic questions that can dramatically improve the power of an individual's tactical actions.

Adherence to the rule of silence is difficult for some people, especially sales and marketing personnel. It is one thing to accept intellectually the value of a question–answer format; it is another thing to demonstrate the discipline to do it. I once attended an executive review where the vice president of sales became so outraged when he could not share anecdotal success stories that his face grew purple-red, he

The Corrective Action Form

Window 1: Gap	**Window 2:** Pareto Analysis
• Does the historical data exhibit a trend? • Is the trend favorable or unfavorable? • Is the gap narrowing or widening? • Are there cyclical trends? • Which aberrations require analysis? • Will we meet the end-of-cycle goal? • How does this measure affect other parts of the business?	• Does the data suggest a focus? • How can we further segment the data? By region, product family, customer, age? • Can we do a further Pareto within a Pareto? • What is the quantitative impact of fixing this focal area?
Window 4: Corrective Actions	**Window 3:** Root Cause Analysis
• Is there at least one corrective action for each root cause? • Do corrective actions advance the quality of the root cause analysis? • Are there too many corrective actions? Choose the vital few. • Will they close the gap? Assess the quantitative impact of corrective actions? • Do the actions go beyond events to set new standardized procedures? • What additional efforts are needed? • Do these corrective actions tie to a revised calendar schedule or action plan? • Do these corrective actions align with other activities?	• Is the fishbone analysis detailed enough? • Did you use a team to create the fishbone? • Are there too many 'vital' root causes? • Are these root causes symptoms of a more fundamental problem? • On what data do you base your conclusions? • What charts support your conclusions? • Why did you fail to predict this problem? • Did your PDPC predict this problem? • How can we improve the way we set targets like this in the future?

Verify: As a team, do we believe that these corrective actions are necessary and sufficient to close the gap and sustain improvement?

Future Implications:

- What are you trying to accomplish in the next review period?
- What might go wrong?
- What countermeasures did you put into place to keep on plan?

FIGURE 8-2 Ask Questions to Improve the Power of Corrective Actions

verbally attacked others who were practicing the "new way," and he threatened not to return. In a most gentle and persistent way, the other executives worked with this man to understand that there are other venues for presentations. If the group is satisfied with the quality of this man's corrective actions and rigor of his causal analysis, and if he displays no significant gaps in performance, then they do not need to hear about trade show experiences, motivational stories, and the other positive details of his function—at that particular meeting. There are many other opportunities apart from the group monthly strategy review to share these insights and stories.

ACCELERATE STRUCTURAL CHANGES

When the root cause analysis is thorough and concise, no one needs to explain conclusions or corrective actions. Rather, the corrective action analysis reads like a memo, and the review proceeds quickly.

When a gap analysis is weak or confusing, however, peers energetically work to improve the quality and quantitative impact of the individual's corrective actions. This is not a free-for-all discussion. Rather, it is a controlled factual dialogue that reinforces the root cause problem-solving process. Peers offer new facts to test hypotheses, challenge false assumptions, improve weak strategies, and provide additional resource support. Such a fact-based dialogue creates a highly focused energetic social environment to generate on-the-spot improvements to corrective actions.

The result is an electrifying experience. Some people worry that a monthly peer review will discourage and depress people. Quite the opposite is true. When people rapidly see and test the impact of current strategies, they wake up. They shift from inertia to informed action. When faced with predictions that did not come true, human beings naturally search for the reasons why. They cannot help but respond to fresh factual data. They care and become engaged as enthusiastic scientists actively searching for the satisfaction of the "ahas." The result is a focused *transforming* experience reaching far beyond any one individual's abilities.

BEING ON PLAN ISN'T GOOD ENOUGH

Some people think that by setting low annual goals and expectations, they will never have any misses and avoid public exposure. In some settings, however, this waves a red flag. Some leaders warn their subordinates that when they see no misses, they know that the organization is not stretching. They want to see an occasional miss. So, it is not uncommon for a leader to stop a meeting and insist that an individual elevate his or her year-end target.

What is the best percentage of deviations or "red lights"? Many people initially guess "none" or maybe "1 percent." But such a management philosophy only institutionalizes mediocrity; it does not permit people to fail. A challenging breakthrough may exhibit 30 to 40 percent monthly deviations from expectation. However, when people discuss them thoroughly and adjust tactical plans accordingly, they often achieve more dramatic progress than those with a seemingly attractive 95 percent success rate.

VERTICALLY SEQUENCE THE REVIEWS, BOTTOM UP

Peer reviews can dramatically accelerate any change process. But just because one team gains a valuable lesson does not guarantee that the entire organization will learn the same lesson or function in a coordinated fashion. Local problems may emerge from the effects of a solution installed by another group. And different groups may concurrently develop different solutions. Working independently, no single group can confront the false assumptions and operating norms of the larger organization or align improvement activities.

To facilitate knowledge exchange *among* groups, some leaders install structured procedures to sequence the vertical and horizontal flow of vital information. Specifically, they design and control the monthly peer review as a *multitiered* process. What does this look like? Each month, team reviews start at the project level and roll up to the senior level. Level by level, teams report upward any gaps that require the support, help, or influence of others. The choreography of hierarchical reviews continually aligns the numerous change efforts throughout the organization consistent with the linked objectives developed and cascaded during the "catchball" process for deployment.

Whatever the design and sequence of the reviews, the important things are to

- publish a review schedule;
- stick to the review schedule;
- create a positive learning climate;
- track deviations from plan;
- challenge the causal analysis;
- verify vertical linkage among the reviews.

The power of frequent vertical monthly reviews is that it does not lock the organization into a plan that is not working. If anyone discovers a failure during the implementation phase, then he or she can modify the initial plan and communicate these changes up and down the organization.

PRACTICE AND REWARD GOOD PLANNING AND REVIEW PRACTICES

Monkey see, monkey do. If you skip the review, your subordinates will too. This is especially true for the executive team. As the executive team learns how to conduct effective reviews, so will the rest of the organization.

Rapid strategy deployment requires full attendance at group monthly reviews. In other words, the group monthly review takes priority over all other daily management activities. After all, what can be more important than the priority gaps for breakthrough performance? Scheduled in advance, written into the monthly calendar, the group monthly review is a dedicated time that other activities get scheduled around.

Who attends the monthly review? The same two levels of the hierarchy that negotiated the plan. This is what we mean by a *standardized* review process. The bowling charts, corrective action forms, and action plans are updated every month at all levels of the organization. Any employee can attend any department's monthly review, including those conducted at the executive level, and immediately grasp the key issues. The rhythmic protocol, the choreography of the meeting, is the same.

BOX: Use Peer Review to Accelerate "Right" Action

- Focus only on deviations from prediction
- Abolish presentations
- Begin with a brief and controlled silence
- Challenge the rigor of the causal analysis
- Separate fact from fiction
- Verify the impact of corrective actions
- Being on plan is not good enough
- Vertically sequence the reviews
- Standardize the best review practices

SUMMARY

Rapid strategy implementation requires more than a set of annual objectives, motivated individuals, and frequent review. It requires the ability to rapidly identify and respond to sensitive changes in the environment within the current planning cycle and across the years to keep people aligned with the plan and the plan aligned with changes in the environment. In short, rapid strategy deployment concerns itself not with static entities but with the active process of *organizing*. This is a continuous process, with no beginning and no end, that links one year to the next in a multiyear planned transformation toward a continually evolving vision. In the next and last chapter, we will learn how to conduct an annual review to evaluate and improve the effectiveness of our *entire* planning and review process as we stretch toward our long-term objectives with increasing speed and accuracy.

CHAPTER 9

HOW CAN WE CONDUCT AN ANNUAL REVIEW?

EXAMINE AND IMPROVE COLLECTIVE BEHAVIOR

The monthly review is a transforming process—one intended to achieve stated goals and objectives. Yet, sometimes we make discoveries during the planning cycle that can affect our decisions and strategies in future planning cycles. From year to year, we can use this added intelligence to improve the plan and our planning skills. The more rapidly we identify any planning and execution weaknesses, the more quickly we can modify our behavior to advance toward our midterm strategies and long-term vision.

To improve their ability to execute any plan, wise leaders conduct a formal process to detect, analyze, and reflect on the quality of their plan and their planning skills. On an annual basis, they document, review, and improve their collective ability to

- *focus* on the vital few strategic accomplishments;
- *align* people, resources, and methods with these priorities;
- *control* the implementation details; and

- *evaluate* the reliability and effectiveness of the targeting process.

Such disciplined activity improves their agility and power to achieve any and all desired outcomes.

PLANNING AND IMPLEMENTATION IS A REPEATABLE PROCESS

Many people think of strategic planning as an event or a stand-alone process, separate from the budgeting or review process.However, rapid reliable results require that leaders define and manage a set of interconnected processes that control the direction of the organization. The monthly review is only one part of this larger planning and implementation process. Other parallel supporting processes include

- identifying critical changes in the environment,
- refreshing the vision and long-term direction,
- choosing the vital mid-term breakthroughs,
- sequencing annual stretch goals,
- selecting daily management priorities,
- aligning individual and department goals with strategic priorities,
- modifying the business systems to achieve new levels of performance, and
- increasing reliability and effectiveness of the targeting process.

These activities are not mere calendar events or isolated planning meetings. Rather, they form repeatable steps in an annual planning and implementation *process* to achieve long-term objectives. Although the annual planning and implementation steps initially appear in sequential order, these activities form a set of interrelated processes that proceed concurrently throughout the year.

THREE TECHNIQUES IMPROVE THE RELIABILITY OF THE TARGETING PROCESS

Like any other process, the planning and implementation process can be documented, standardized, and continually improved. Key steps include the following:

- *Document* all aspects of the planning, implementation, and review process including key planning steps, the planning calendar, methods and criteria for each step of the planning cycle, review protocols, priority objectives, and assumptions about cause and effect.
- *Standardize* the planning and review process to reduce variation in vocabulary, planning forms, alignment protocols, decision-making process, frequency of review, reporting format, group protocols, and other tools and techniques.
- *Continuously reduce delays* to get faster at detecting critical changes in the environment, setting and communicating new targets, deploying resources, adapting methods to meet new requirements, and eliminating deviations from plan.

These activities keep the organization aligned with the plan and the plan aligned with changes in the environment. Such a dynamic organization is called a *learning organization*, or more accurately an "unlearning" organization, where coworkers openly confront ineffective behaviors and undesirable outcomes to replace them quickly with more desirable ones in the spirit of continuous improvement.

MAP YOUR CURRENT PLANNING AND IMPLEMENTATION PROCESS

To identify initial improvement opportunities, wise leaders make explicit the simple components of their existing planning and deployment process. This information can be displayed in a macro process flow chart. Figure 9-1 illustrates a simple annual planning and implementation process.

A well-designed planning and implementation process is a continuous cycle with no beginning and no end. The input is a set of critical changes in the environment and the current organizational system. The output is a transformed business system that detects and thrives on these critical changes. The steps between map how the organization unlearns old familiar behaviors, acquires new capabilities, and reflects on the speed of its adaptability. The result is a *double loop learning system* that keeps the plan aligned with the environment and daily activity aligned with the plan.

Each company can and should tailor its planning and implementation process to reflect its culture and teachings. However, effective targeting processes exhibit some common success factors worth mentioning: priorities, a customer-focused plan, a two-track planning process to achieve breakthroughs *and* improve operational excellence, an experimental learning process, teamwork, an explicit hierarchical linkage, strategy control measures, frequent reviews, a process orientation, and an annual planning calendar. These features help create a reliable targeting process for competitive advantage.

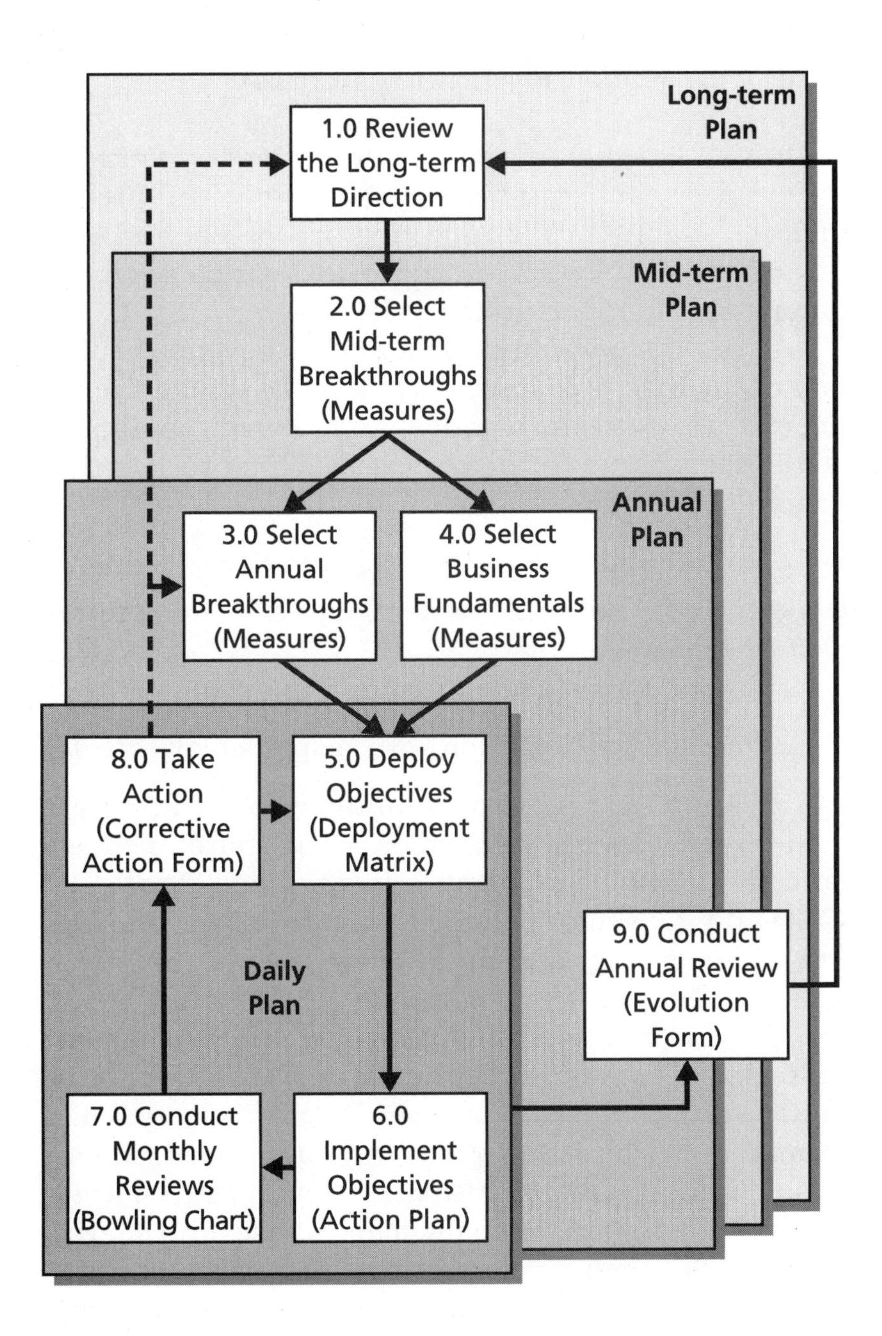

FIGURE 9-1 Create a Repeatable Annual Planning Cycle
Source: Michele Bechtell, *The Management Compass* (Blackhall Publishing, Dublin, 1995).

MAP THE ANNUAL PLANNING CALENDAR

Although many companies adopt similar planning principles, each company engages in a unique sequence of activities, supporting processes, and timing. These routine activities provides a rich source of improvement opportunities.

An annual planning calendar goes beyond the theory of the macro process map to make visible the architecture, pattern, balance, and flow of the annual activities unique to the company. This process flow map displays the

- actual planning and implementation activities;
- calendar schedule to develop, negotiate, and review detailed plans;
- key inputs and deliverables; and
- levels of participation with responsible parties.

It shows how all the planning systems integrate and ensures that key activities occur simultaneously and sequentially to form a repeatable process. The CEO and the senior team are responsible for developing, distributing, and monitoring this annual planning calendar.

A review of the annual planning and deployment calendar will reveal numerous improvement opportunities such as missing or out-of sequence steps, disconnects with other planning and management systems, inadequate participation, inaccurate information, and delays. A calendar map exposes the contradictions between common sense and what we do as well as the gaps between what we believe we are doing and our factual behavior.

The annual planning calendar is simple to create, control, and improve. Some simple steps include the

BOX: Conduct an Annual Audit

1. Evaluate the results—progress toward the annual and mid-term objectives.
   - Which targets were missed and why?
   - What are the root barriers to accomplishing our objectives?
   - To what extent were prior strategies deployed throughout the organization?
2. Evaluate the process- the organization's skill at planning
   - How accurate is the annual planning calendar?
   - Which best practices will we standardize? What went RIGHT when we achieved expected results?
   - Where can we improve the organization's planning system?
3. Modify the planning and implementation system to reflect lessons.
   - How will we improve the next planning cycle?
   - How will we modify the annual planning calendar?
   - How do we incorporate incomplete objectives into the next planning cycle?
4. Report the weakness assessment upward to the next hierarchical level.

following: Give the planning process a special name with concise definition; specify the length of the planning cycle such as six months or a year; map the current process as it exists today, with months running across the top and levels of hierarchy on the side; conduct a group review to locate improvement opportunities; create an improved flow chart; and transfer the dates from the new planning flow chart to a daily calendar and distribute to all employees.

CREATE A FIELD MANUAL OF "BEST" PRACTICES

The macro process map and annual calendar make visible the key steps in the planning cycle. However, they do not specify the practical details. They do not document the ground rules, techniques, and tools necessary for the successful completion of each step.

To further reduce unwanted variability and develop consistent methods, some companies create a customized strategy deployment field manual. They use this workbook to document, teach, and continually improve the "best" planning, implementation, and review techniques. The workbook does not describe theory. Rather, it documents the recommended and expected protocols. A practical reference, it organizes in one place the requirements, forms, and ground rules for each step in the planning cycle.

One easy format follows the steps in the macro process flow chart. A table of contents outlines each of the main steps of the targeting process, such as "Select annual breakthroughs" or "Conduct monthly reviews." Seven main steps in the targeting process would mean seven chapters. Then, chapter by chapter, the field guide describes a reliable miniprocess including the key leadership challenge, the standards, ground rules, and vocabulary to complete the step, a standard form to document the conclusions of the step, and a place to list opportunities to improve this step in the future.

A living, breathing leadership tool, the field manual is often released in annual editions to reflect various improvements identified during the annual audit. As members discover, reach consensus on, and standardize new practices that increase reliability and speed, the field manual will reflect these changes.

CONDUCT SITE VISITS

The macro planning process map documents the logical activities that produce results. The annual planning calendar specifies the deadlines and deliverables. The field manual documents the protocols and procedures for completing each step. But how exactly do members of the organization modify these standards over time?

The answer is an annual company-wide self-assessment. Prior to setting new objectives, leaders at every level of the organization candidly evaluate their adherence to agreed-on protocols and their problem-solving skills. They systematically review each step of the planning and implementation process to standardize the best practices, identify improvement opportunities, and make recommendations and changes. Then they report upward the results of their weakness assessment. The intent is to disseminate learning, the problems and corrective actions, and to improve the overall reliability of the targeting process.

At the heart of the annual self-assessment is the plan-do-check-act cycle for continuous improvement. Level by level and step by step, coworkers investigate: How well did we *plan* what we said we wanted to accomplish last time? Did we *do* what we said we would do? Did we routinely *check* progress along the way? Did we *act* on discrepancies in a timely fashion? Reviewed once, these four questions provide leadership insight. Year after year, they provide a reliable mechanism to continually improve results.

Site visits remain the CEO's responsibility and cannot be delegated. Starting at the lowest level, the CEO sequentially reviews factual performance and the weakness assessment. The site visit is *not* a check of results. Rather, it is a check of the *process* used to achieve the results. The intent is to evaluate the extent to which priorities were deployed and implemented in each organization and to identify generic improvement opportunities. Level by level, the CEO listens to self-evaluations as workers report on the following topics:

- *Outcomes: What are the current vision gaps*? Peers report remaining gaps and the causes of *disappointing results* such as nonadherence to plan, poor strategies, and/or moving targets.
- *Process: How consistent and reliable were our planning and implementation behaviors*? Peers report *variable process behaviors* such as failing to adhere to the planning calendar, follow agreed-on review protocols, integrate all necessary business units, follow a root cause decision-making process, or systematically improve the planning and implementation process.
- Direction*: What new developments alter our direction or change our objectives*? Peers evaluate their slow response to new developments including their failure to detect new or emerging issues, reach consensus on the critical changes in direction, translate the vision into measures of success, or isolate the breakthrough priorities.

The third step links the annual audit back to the strategic planning process described at the beginning of this book.

DOCUMENT THE HISTORICAL IMPROVEMENTS

Seeing improvement opportunities and taking corrective action are two different things. For this reason, wise leaders codify their new knowledge in two types of improved procedures. Specifically, they take the time to reach consensus on two points:

- Which best practices will we standardize? *What went right when we achieved expected results*?
- How will we improve the targeting system in the next planning cycle? *What new behaviors will minimize failed objectives*?

The answers to these questions cause the planning, implementation, and review protocols to evolve over time. In the first year, individuals may not chart particularly well, choose weak measurement systems, or struggle with root cause decision-making techniques. In the second year, the leadership may take steps to improve the process for creating realistic action plans. The third year, they may take on the challenge to deploy more deeply into the organization. At all times, the focus is on the performance of the planning process, not the individual. This conclusion step in the annual audit focuses leadership attention on

BOX: Make Annual Planning a Reliable Process

- Map your current planning and implementation process
- Study, standardize and improve the factual behaviors
- Create and distribute an annual planning and implementation calendar
- Publish and distribute a field manual of "best practices"
- Conduct site visits to verify and improve collective behavior
- Document the vital few annual system improvements and remaining challenges

the *few* most important opportunities for continued improvement. The CEO is responsible for tracking and updating this vital information.

To focus leadership attention on the remaining challenges, some leaders document the conclusions of their weakness assessment. They use a one-page form to summarize the lessons and material improvements in the targeting process. At one glance, everyone can see the historical development of the planning and review process. For each fiscal year, they document the vital few structural changes and remaining challenges.

CONCLUSION

In the early years of adopting a formal planning, implementation, and review system, many people will have to overcome many fears. The leadership will succeed to the extent that it creates a review *system* that evaluates the performance of the planning and review process, not simply the performance of the individual. As members of the organization gain confidence in the review process, they will experience a dramatic increase in energy, focus, and contribution. Safe and open conditions encourage people to improve continually the quality of plans and the review process.

Learning the principles and mechanics for rapid strategy implementation is like learning to ride a bike. The first few times, most children concentrate on climbing onto the seat of the bike, stretching their feet to reach the pedals. When they can successfully mount the bike, they immediately focus on staying on the bike, controlling the handlebars, and pushing the pedals to gain forward motion. When they fall off and skin their knees, they get back up again. One day they no longer focus on the *mechanics* of riding the bike. Rather, they focus only on their *destination.*

They have become familiar and adept with this transport mechanism.

A structured review process is a transportation tool. The first year may feel awkward as people struggle to apply causal analysis to every deviation, silently review the rigor of peer contributions, and align individual plans. However, it is worth it in the end. You will experience significant gains by taking the time to align individual goals, increase the frequency of review, and consistently apply causal analysis to gaps in annual goals. As people gain confidence in the tools, techniques, and mechanics described in these pages, they will make rapid strides toward the vision. They will experience a dramatic increase in energy, focus, and contribution.

In the end, rapid strategy implementation is not magic, mystery, or miracle. It is method! And it can be learned, just like exemplary leadership.

BOX: How to Conduct Frequent Effective Business Reviews

- Choose what to review
- Identify the critical few annual priorities
- Assign and align individual contributions
- Develop a detailed action plan.
- Conduct frequent reviews
- Track deviations from expectation.
- Identify root barriers to progress.
- Install timely appropriate corrective action.
- Standardize the "best" review practices
- Define and enforce recommended behaviors.
- Verify the impact of corrective actions.
- Conduct an annual audit to evaluate and improve collective behavior

INDEX

A

D

F

T

U

V

ABOUT THE AUTHOR

Michele L. Bechtell is a global business authority on customer focus, rapid strategy deployment, and large-scale organizational change. With over twenty years consulting experience, and ten years in private practice, she helps executives re-direct their organizations to build and sustain competitive advantage, aligning people, activities, and resources with strategic intent.

Prior to founding her private consulting practice, Ms. Bechtell worked as a senior consultant for Arthur D. Little, Inc., an international consulting firm, and The Forum Corporation, an international executive training company. She also served as a faculty member of the Arthur D. Little School of Management, a leading international graduate school that awards the Master of Science in Management degree. There she taught total quality management, process improvement, and organizational behavior. She served as

Director of the International Human Resource Development Program and Director of advanced management studies for the Hariri Foundation.

A seasoned author and engaging speaker, Ms. Bechtell educates business leaders on proven methods to accomplish breakthrough objectives. Her third book, *On Target* (Berrett-Koehler) shows how to conduct powerful business reviews to accelerate change and achieve quantum leaps in performance. Her second book, *The Management Compass* (Blackhall Publishing), describes a reliable strategy implementation process called hoshin planning to achieve strategic breakthroughs. Her first book, *Untangling Organizational Gridlock* (Blackhall Publishing) won the Golden Quill Award from the American Society for Quality Control and describes the basic principles of total quality management and large-scale organizational change.

Educator and strategy consultant, Bechtell has assisted some of the largest most successful companies around the world to develop the leadership capabilities to focus, align, and control any plan to accomplish ambitious objectives. The success of her many engagements reflects her extensive experience with adult learning, the design of technical training materials, and the successful architecture of large-scale change.

Ms. Bechtell holds a Master of Science degree from Cornell University in the School of Industrial and Labor Relations, and a Bachelor of Arts degree in mathematics from Bowdoin College. She resides with her husband in historic antebellum Madison, Georgia near Atlanta. You can reach her at **mbechtell@prodigy.net.**

Also by Michele Bechtell

The Management Compass

How Wise Leaders Control the Strategy Implementation Process

Second Edition

To create competitive advantage, many leaders design strategic plans and strategy scorecards only to discover they lack the means to implement any plan. In this bestselling book, Michele L. Bechtell shows that strategy implementation is a PROCESS, not a paper plan or set of measures. She encourages leaders to study the predictable behaviors that produce predictable results. In six chapters, you will learn how companies like Hewlett-Packard, Intel, Motorola, Procter & Gamble, and Texas Instruments minimize errors and delays in all aspects of their strategic planning and implementation process. Specifically, you will learn how to define, control, and improve your focusing process, alignment process, transforming process, and review process. This reliable self-correcting strategy management system, sometimes called hoshin management or policy deployment, keeps the plan aligned with changes in the environment and activities aligned with the plan to deliver consistently superior results.

Hardcover • ISBN 1-842180-43-6 • $24.95

Untangling Organizational Gridlock

Strategies for Building a Customer Focus

To survive today's dynamic environment, many leaders do similar "good" things: they conduct market research, train personnel, advocate process control, and empower teams to improve quality, cost, and speed. Yet too often performance declines and prior targets become moving targets. Winner of the Golden Quill Award, this book shows how to thrive in a dynamic marketplace. Dividing the book into two parts, Michele L. Bechtell shows how to create an agile enterprise that profitably responds to rapid changes in the environment. Part I describes five principles or imperatives for operational excellence, sometimes called total quality management, that sharpen all aspects of the enterprise and guide every successful strategy and implementation. Part II describes the little-known technology of large-scale organizational change. In five chapters, readers learn how to design a successful architecture for organizational change that pays attention to the things we do AND the order in which we do them. If you have tried and failed to achieve total quality, seek to create a common culture in a merger or acquisition, or are "going global," this book is a must-read. It describes the technology for change that enables organizations to not simply survive but thrive on change.

Hardcover • ISBN 1-842180-44-4 • $29.95

Berrett-Koehler Publishers

BERRETT-KOEHLER is an independent publisher of books, periodicals, and other publications at the leading edge of new thinking and innovative practice on work, business, management, leadership, stewardship, career development, human resources, entrepreneurship, and global sustainability.

Since the company's founding in 1992, we have been committed to supporting the movement toward a more enlightened world of work by publishing books, periodicals, and other publications that help us to integrate our values with our work and work lives, and to create more humane and effective organizations.

We have chosen to focus on the areas of work, business, and organizations, because these are central elements in many people's lives today. Furthermore, the work world is going through tumultuous changes, from the decline of job security to the rise of new structures for organizing people and work. We believe that change is needed at all levels—individual, organizational, community, and global—and our publications address each of these levels.

We seek to create new lenses for understanding organizations, to legitimize topics that people care deeply about but that current business orthodoxy censors or considers secondary to bottom-line concerns, and to uncover new meaning, means, and ends for our work and work lives.

See next page for other publications
from Berrett-Koehler

Other books from Berrett-Koehler Publishers

Profit Building
Cutting Costs Without Cutting People

Perry Ludy

Cultivating a loyal, productive workforce is crucial to business success. In *Profit Building,* Perry Ludy—who has worked for top companies in every major field from manufacturing to retail—introduces a five-step process called the PBP (Profit Building Process), which offers specific techniques for improving profitability by stimulating creative thinking and motivating teams to work together more effectively.

Hardcover, 200 pages • ISBN 1-57675-108-2 • Item #51082-402 $27.95

The Knowledge Engine
How to Create Fast Cycles of Knowledge-to-Performance and Performance-to-Knowledge

Lloyd Baird and John C. Henderson

The Knowledge Engine shows that in the new economy, knowledge must be captured from performance as it is happening and used to improve the next round of performance, integrating learning and performance into a continuous cycle. The authors show how to produce knowledge as part of the work process and quickly apply that learning back to performance to create a "knowledge engine" that drives ongoing performance improvement and adds value in every area of your organization.

Hardcover, 200 pages • ISBN 1-57675-104-X • Item #5104X-402 $27.95

Lean and Green

Pamela J. Gordon

No longer will managers think they have to choose between doing the right thing for the planet and doing well in business. This this book gives hundreds of examples—at well known organizations including Sony, IBM, Polaroid, Intel, and Louisiana-Pacific—in which a lean and successful operation comes from making green decisions.

Paperback, 250 pages • ISBN 1-57675-170-8 • Item #51708-402 $24.95

Berrett-Koehler Publishers
PO Box 565, Williston, VT 05495-9900
Call toll-free! **800-929-2929** 7 am-12 midnight

Or fax your order to 802-864-7627
For fastest service order online: **www.bkconnection.com**